Buying and Supplying Quality

Also available from Quality Press

Procurement Quality Control, Fourth Edition
ASQC Customer-Supplier Technical Committee;
James L. Bossert, editor

Supplier Certification: A Continuous Improvement Strategy
Richard A. Maass, John O. Brown, and James L. Bossert

To request a complimentary catalog of publications, call
800-248-1946.

Buying and Supplying Quality

Richard T. Weber
Ross H. Johnson

ASQC Quality Press
Milwaukee, Wisconsin

Buying and Supplying Quality
Richard T. Weber and Ross H. Johnson

Library of Congress Cataloging-in-Publication Data

Weber, Richard T.
    Buying and supplying quality / Richard T. Weber, Ross H. Johnson.
  —2nd ed.
      p. cm.
    On previous ed. Ross H. Johnson's name appeared first on t.p.
    Rev. ed. of: Buying quality. c1988.
    Includes bibliographical references and index.
    ISBN 0-87389-253-4
    1. Quality control.   I. Johnson, Ross H.   II. Johnson, Ross H.
Buying quality.   III. Title.
    TS156.W38   1993
    658.5'62—dc20   93-24982
                                                      CIP

10 9 8 7 6 5 4 3 2 1

ISBN 0-87389-253-4

Acquisitions Editor: Susan Westergard
Production Editor: Annette Wall
Marketing Administrator: Mark Olson
Set in Times and Helvetica Condensed by Montgomery Media, Inc.
Cover design by Montgomery Media, Inc.
Printed and bound by BookCrafters, Inc.

ASQC Mission: To facilitate continuous improvement and increase customer satisfaction by identifying, communicating, and promoting the use of quality principles, concepts, and technologies; and thereby be recognized throughout the world as the leading authority on, and champion for, quality.

For a free copy of the ASQC Quality Press Publications Catalog, including ASQC membership information, call 800-248-1946.

Printed in the United States of America

  Printed on acid-free recycled paper

ASQC
Quality Press
611 East Wisconsin Avenue
Milwaukee, Wisconsin 53202

Contents

Strategy for Obtaining Quality from Suppliers

Chapter 1

W hen establishing ways of doing business with suppliers, a company must consider its goals and objectives and understand how a supplier relationship can contribute or detract from overall company profitability and stability. A strategy for obtaining quality products and services from suppliers (sometimes referred to as vendors or contractors) needs to be an integral part of overall company strategy. Once a company recognizes the importance of quality as a part of strategy in achieving company goals and objectives, the role of quality in supplier strategy also becomes apparent. The many tactics discussed later all fit into the strategic plan, thus contributing to the overall company. Since suppliers have a large impact on the production operation in a company, they also have an impact on profitability, overall schedules, costs, and product quality. Thus, a company needs to maximize the number of supplier-related activities over which it has control and minimize the number over which it does not. We are not saying, however, that the company needs to tell the supplier exactly how to do things; instead, it should adopt a strategy in which it assigns responsibilities where they belong. This includes assignment of responsibilities within one's own company as well as properly defining and monitoring those responsibilities assigned to the supplier.

In today's society, our lives, livelihood, and schedules depend upon the satisfactory performance and operation of products and services supplied to us as customers. In meeting their obligations to their own customers, companies likewise depend on the performance and quality of items procured from suppliers. More and more companies are recognizing the importance of this interrelationship and are incorporating quality objectives and supplier strategies into overall company strategy.

Elements of Strategy

The final judge of the success of a strategy is the marketplace. The customer will respond by purchasing those products with greatest perceived value. In cases where the use life of a product is short—such as food, household supplies, or other frequently purchased items—the perceived quality can be based on fitness for use perceived from prior purchases of the product. With longer-life items such as home appliances or automobiles, the perceived value is based more on other factors. These factors relate back to the quality strategy of the manufacturer, which must determine customer satisfiers and how customers distinguish good products from poor ones.

In the diagnosis of any strategic problem, we can divide the elements into *controllable actions*—those under company control—and *uncontrollable events*—those not under company control, such as competitor's actions, consumer thinking, and government policies. It would be a mistake for a company to assume that supplier actions are not under buyer control. Subsequent chapters will define the many ways in which a company can control the quality of purchased goods.

We will also discuss the substantial impact of supplier quality on in-plant productivity and on future business of the company.

Purchasing Strategy

Purchasing strategy is part of company strategy. In carrying out company strategy, it is necessary for purchasing managers to

- understand the purchasing environment.
- anticipate and monitor changes in the environment.
- work closely with suppliers or potential suppliers, facilitating the exchange of information.
- identify threats and opportunities related to purchasing objectives.
- identify the firm's strengths and weaknesses in light of the current environment.
- define and analyze strategic alternatives.
- select courses of action applicable to the company and its products.

Concurrent with the above steps, it is necessary to

- identify critical materials based on threats to supply.
- identify critical purchases based on difficult requirements.
- consider long-term and short-term needs.

Quality and Strategy

To deal with quality and strategy, it is necessary to delve into some differing interpretations of the term *quality*. Quality is sometimes defined as conformance to specifications and fitness for use. Some marketing texts, however, in using the term, would say that the Cadillac is a higher-quality automobile than the Chevrolet. The intended meaning is that the Cadillac has greater performance expectations or, in other words, is more luxurious. Another meaning of quality is more subjective, involving quality as perceived by the customer, whose failure to perceive the desired quality results in reduced sales of the product. A firm, in defining its strategy, must deal with each of the concepts separately—and together as a composite strategy.

Quality and Productivity

In past years, quality was often viewed in opposition to productivity—that is, increasing quality reduced productivity. This fallacy has hindered quality improvement in many companies. More recent experience shows the reverse to be true. We see that as quality increases, so does productivity. The key is the point at which productivity is measured. The traditional practice was to measure productivity at the end of the production line. A more realistic measure includes customer acceptance of products; in other words, products returned by the customer are subtracted from productivity figures. As a result, acceptable quality becomes a key factor in increasing productivity. Dr. Armand V. Feigenbaum,[1] widely recognized quality control authority, speaks of the "hidden factory capacity" required to do repair and rework, in some cases up to 30 percent of the normal plant capacity. If rework and repair were eliminated, the additional capacity (space and employees) would be available to perform productive work.

- As defects decrease, yield increases.
- Making it right the first time eliminates rejects and rework.
- Placing responsibility for quality on the operator removes the need for inspection. An operator is trained to accept full responsibility for quality in his or her work.

Further evidence that quality and productivity go hand in hand comes from successful foreign business in the United States. Some of

---

[1] Armand V. Feigenbaum. *Total Quality Control* (New York: McGraw-Hill 1983), 46.

these businesses are more successful than our own, yet they use similar people. Management emphasis and employee involvement make the difference.

Productivity and Suppliers
These concepts also apply to the purchasing operation.

- As rejections decrease, costs of procurement decrease, as do delays in production.
- Selecting the right supplier and correctly writing the purchase order eliminates renegotiation, changes, and rejections.
- Purchasing agents and buyers are trained to accept responsibility for quality along with price and delivery. Quality is not viewed as the responsibility of "someone else."

Some executives define productivity as increased output for a given input. Too often, the output is measured at the end of the production line, or at the shipping dock. This concept of productivity fails to adequately consider quality. In its broadest sense, the measure of productivity must only include high-quality products that meet customers' needs. A manager cannot say a productivity goal was achieved if products are later returned by customers or a product recall occurs due to product deficiencies.

A supplier's view of productivity is one measure of the supplier's program and serves as a good indicator of what might be expected in products supplied. Those companies recognizing that improvement of productivity is a by-product of quality improvement are more likely to supply products that meet requirements.

Products meeting requirements are more likely to come from companies that are concerned with long-range goals. Some companies place greater emphasis on short-term objectives, especially earnings. In introducing objectives of improved quality, they are likely to expect results too soon and too easily. Achievement of in-house quality and quality in suppliers' product occurs only over time; it takes patience as well as skill.

Some companies that have been hit hardest by competitors, such as manufacturers of automobiles and TV sets, have adopted concepts and strategies popularized by the Japanese. Many firms that are not yet affected may still be too complacent about quality. Quality experts point out that the Japanese effort was a nationwide effort over a fifteen- to twenty-year period. U.S. companies trying to incorporate these concepts may find that it takes longer than a few months or even a few years to achieve improved quality.

Quality and Quality Control

A quality product does not just come about without special effort. Quality control refers to all the activities that must be carried out to achieve the quality product. Sometimes the term *quality program* or *quality control system* is used to refer to this set of activities that ensure that the product conforms to the standards set for it and thus meets the user's needs. Quality control represents a broad-based function. There is usually a quality control department, but all parts of an organization have important roles to perform toward this end. This need for a broad-based approach will be examined in detail later when we look closely at a buyer carrying out his responsibilities.

Sources of Poor Quality

Any company has four primary sources of inadequate quality: (1) inadequate emphasis by management on quality, (2) inadequate definition of product or its intended use, (3) defects introduced due to in-house causes, and (4) defects originating in purchased items, materials, or processes. The fourth category would include defects originating in items supplied by other plants of the same company. The fact that the source is part of the same company does not usually make a difference in our approach to quality achievement. Quality problems often arise because of different goals, different locations, different people, or involvement with different lines of products. In this book, suppliers are defined as makers of goods produced in any separate facility.

Excuses for Poor Quality

Much has been stated about the Japanese' success in achievement of quality in their products. Perhaps this success should be viewed as a setback in the salability of U.S. products in world markets. On the other hand, we are told that we should attempt to learn and apply the techniques the Japanese employ. Those making these statements have forgotten (or do not realize) that these techniques were taught to the Japanese by people from this country, such as Drs. Deming and Juran. The message they brought to the Japanese was to emphasize quality. The techniques they used were also available to U.S. firms. In other words, the technical capability for production of good quality made available through the knowledge of our quality experts was accepted and has sometimes been better utilized by the Japanese over the past thirty or more years.

Some say the culture of the Japanese permits them to better apply these quality concepts. However, in the 1930s, "Made in Japan" was a symbol of poor quality. Today, in 1993, that same phrase is a symbol of high quality despite little change in Japanese culture during the last seventy years. The idea that culture determines a nation's ability to produce quality products, then, is fallacious. A company that must achieve quality in its products cannot afford to accept such delusions and excuses from its own people or from its suppliers as it pursues its quality objectives. Many U.S. firms have shown that they are technically capable of competing in the production of quality goods for sale in the world markets. Companies that previously held that finance and marketing were key elements of a success strategy are beginning to recognize that product quality can also be a strategic weapon in the competition for worldwide market share.

How a Supplier Views Quality

In dealing with the buyer, a supplier responds to those factors perceived to be of greatest importance. If the buyer places emphasis upon cost and schedule in negotiating a purchase order, the supplier will perceive these to be of greater importance than other factors, such as service and quality. The inclusion of quality requirements in the contract is important, and the buyer who is knowledgeable in quality and who stresses quality to the supplier along with price and delivery will in the long run be rewarded with greater quality efforts on the part of the supplier and fewer problems on the contract.

Defining Quality

A quality product is defined by some people as one that will satisfy the needs and expectations of the customer. Others say that a quality product is one that conforms to the standards established for it. In our prior example's statement that a Cadillac has greater quality than a Chevrolet, this is a different use of the word *quality*. As used in the quality control profession, the term *quality* applies to either of these automobiles or any other products if they conform to the standards (or requirements) established for them. This holds true as long as these standards result in a product that meets the needs of the user. We might then conclude that quality means fitness for intended use or reasonable use. We might also define *quality* as its total value or ability in satisfying the customer from a performance, appearance, durability, and cost standpoint.

An understanding of the meaning of quality is important as it applies to products and purchased materials. Quality consists of many properties of the product. Each of these properties or characteristics must be defined so that quality can be measured and achieved consistently. It is not satisfactory to speak of quality only in terms of good or bad. In the case of purchased items, the definitions of the required quality characteristics must be such that the supplier can know what is wanted and that both the supplier and the using company can measure to determine whether the quality characteristics have been achieved. These needed characteristics should be defined in the purchase order or contract so that both parties know and agree to the requirements. Many characteristics are associated with each product. The following are examples of characteristics that may need to be defined and verified.

1. Physical dimensions
2. Appearance, color, finish, surface roughness
3. Weight, density, porosity, texture, tensile strength
4. Performance or operation
5. Product life and reliability
6. Shelf life, durability, fracture resistance
7. Limits on product's noise or pollutants; freedom from foreign matter or impurity
8. Utility, efficiency, economy in use
9. Ability to be used with other products
10. Ability to perform in specified environments, under certain stresses, or under other use condition such as the presence of heat, cold, moisture, vibration, shock, or radiation
11. Serviceability or ease of repair and maintenance
12. Documentation on product manufacture and testing

The absence of any of these characteristics, where relevant in the manufacture or testing of a product, results in a quality deficiency.

Products or Services

Quality pertains to services as well as products. A substantial proportion of businesses are considered to be service industries, and many contracts or subcontracts involve services. These services can include advertising, contract engineering services, market research, cafeteria services, and repair and maintenance services. As with the purchaser of products, the buyer of services needs to be concerned with price, quality, and schedule considerations. As this book proceeds, we will see that all aspects of a good supplier quality program apply to service contracts as well as contracts for products. Definition of requirements, source selection, and evaluation of what is furnished are as important in the procurement of services as they are in the procurement of tangible items.

The definition of a service, and of the quality characteristics sought in a service, may be more difficult to establish than for a product. This does not mean, however, that careful definition is less important. If the quality and delivery requirements can be closely defined, then the successful bidder can be selected on a price basis. If, however, the company purchasing a service fails to define the quality expected, then the buyer will not be able to define the full scope of the service, and source selection will be more complex. This makes the buyer's job more difficult, since he or she can rely only on knowledge of prior services performed by a supplier, obtained either through direct experience or through reports from others who have used the services.

As with a product, a service must be evaluated in terms of the level of quality plus the degree of consistency, or freedom from excessive variability. Factors affecting variability of service quality can be absenteeism, disruptions to service, service during unexpected breakdowns or adverse weather conditions, and handling of responsibilities under other adverse or unexpected situations.

In summary, the quality considerations in purchasing services are similar to those in purchasing manufactured items. They include establishment of quality standards, evaluation of quality, and assignment of responsibilities.

The benefits of achieved quality and the costs of nonconformance in procuring services are comparable to those encountered in procuring products.

A Company Commitment

In times past, quality was produced by craftsmen relying on simple tools and the skill of their hands. More recently, quality often referred to an after-the-fact evaluation by quality control people of goods produced by the manufacturing people. If items failed to conform, they would be returned to manufacturing to be made right, scrapped if repair was impossible, or in some cases shipped to unknowing customers. In today's more competitive environment, however, concepts such as AQL (acceptable quality level) are no longer sufficient. The management of quality now requires an overall company commitment. Emphasis on quality must be evident in each management action or decision. Each management decision must be reached after careful consideration of its impact on quality. Otherwise, employee attitudes toward quality will reflect management's failure to assign it a higher priority.

The purchasing organization has a heavy responsibility in the pursuit of quality, since the supplier's items have a significant impact on the overall product quality, and the supplier looks to the buyer for direction. Philip Crosby states it well when he says, "Quality improvement is built on getting everyone to do it right the first time."[2] This concept certainly applies to getting the supplier to do it right the first time. The buyer must place emphasis on quality as well as price and schedule. Companies that choose not to demand quality from suppliers, however, may end up being out of business.

> **Case Example.** A supplier was providing a system that included, as a small but critical part, a complex electromechanical unit. When received, the units exhibited various malfunctions. Although the supplier committed during phone conversations to correct the defects, the problems continued. When a quality engineer visited the supplier's facility, he found a good, well-documented quality system, well-trained and knowledgeable inspection personnel, and good product-evaluation techniques. However, throughout the visit the quality engineer detected management emphasis on shipping products to meet delivery schedules rather than quality standards. The quality engineer reported this finding

---

[2] Philip B. Crosby, *Quality Without Tears* (New York: McGraw-Hill, 1984), 59.

to the manager of the purchasing, who worked with the supplier company president to establish the priority of meeting
deliver schedules without any sacrifice of quality.

By placing emphasis on the three primary characteristics in a
procurement—quality, delivery, and cost—the buyer has the negotiating advantage. Even in a single-source situation, the buyer can
achieve an important advantage.

Purchasing Is Vital

The vital interests of any company depend upon the satisfactory performance of products and services rendered by its suppliers.
Deficiencies in supplied products or services can increase spoilage,
reduce sales, delay delivery schedules, and reduce productivity.
These, in turn, adversely affect the company's profits and may even
jeopardize the company's ability to stay in business. Although these
ideas are not new, their importance has become increasingly evident
over the past decade as many U.S. companies have lost large shares
of their market to foreign competitors. This does not mean that price
is any less important than it was in the past but, rather, that buyers and
consumers are paying greater attention to quality as a comparative
factor when selecting products.

The costs of purchased materials, parts, and components make
up a substantial portion of the total direct costs of many companies,
though the proportion varies considerably from company to company and from one product to another within any company. Often
the procured items are complex or perform vital functions in the
product; therefore, purchasers must be sure of the quality of procured items. It is not always easy to obtain this assurance. Since the
manufacturing and quality control operations of the supplier are not
under the direct control or observation of the primary manufacturer
(contractor), it is necessary to implement tasks and controls that will
provide the needed assurance. When a supplier is being considered

for an order, the quality of products supplied previously becomes a primary consideration. If quality has been inadequate and the supplier shows little interest in correcting it, a reorder usually goes to a different supplier. If the reorder is given to a supplier with a record of poor quality, it is as if the supplier is rewarded for poor performance, and the consumer is willing to pay for the bad quality.

The purchasing department has the primary responsibility for administration of the contract with the supplier. Other departments, like engineering and quality control, have the technical know-how about the function of the items and techniques available to ensure a good product. The departments, by working together, can establish a program that will assure that a quality product will be received when scheduled and at a competitive cost.

The Purchasing Function

Many companies can be viewed as performing a conversion process. Their function is to convert raw materials, parts, and/or components (subassemblies) into a product of greater value. For some U.S. companies the procured items and materials constitute more than half the worth of the shipped products. This significant portion of the firm's wealth comes under the control of the purchasing department or purchasing agent. Thus, the procured items must meet the quality and schedule requirements at the right price. If these objectives are met, the purchasing operation contributes to the overall profitability of the company.

> **Case Example.** A supplier was providing a mechanical part that had tight tolerances and critical processing techniques. The parts provided by the supplier were out of tolerance for various reasons and could not be used. Consequently, a production line was shut down. A team including the buyer, a quality engineer, a product engineer, and a tool expert visited the supplier's plant. During the visit, they suggested various corrective actions. The supplier's management agreed to correct the problems but subsequently did not follow

through. A second visit by the same team resulted in additional commitments and the establishment of a sorting operation at incoming inspection to find defective parts. Nevertheless, the problem was eventually solved only by changing suppliers.

Here, a lack of management commitment resulted in loss of a contract. The faster the supplier acts to eliminate and control defects, the less risk of a financial loss.

To ensure the continuity of a company's production operations, the right quantity and quality of procured parts and materials must be available when needed for the manufacturing process. Revised production schedules and shut-down production lines are costly to the company in several ways. Loss of profits, layoff of personnel, and failure to meet customers' delivery dates are serious problems and may lead to loss of sales. While we can, of course, build up inventories of procured material, it is costly to tie up capital in large inventories, and this will not be tolerated by management. Besides, material held in inventory sometimes deteriorates or becomes obsolete due to design changes.

When a purchaser establishes a window of delivery in a twenty-four-hour period and sets penalties such as $5000 per minute for shutting down a production line, a supplier has a strong incentive to comply.

Some U.S. automotive manufacturers, as well as many Japanese firms, have introduced JIT (just-in-time) procurement, wherein supplier items are delivered directly to the production line, and no inventories are maintained. Schedule requirements are provided to the purchasing agent by the production department, and the purchasing agent passes the requirements on to the supplier as part of the subcontract. Similarly, product requirements are defined by engineering and become part of the subcontract. The quality control department may specify additional requirements to assure that the product user's needs are achieved. These quality control requirements, just like the engineering requirements, should also become part of the contract.

The purchasing department must assure that the supplier is capable of meeting all the standards and is committed to meeting them at competitive costs and on schedule.

In carrying out its responsibilities, the purchasing department interrelates with many other parts of the company. Figure 1.1 illustrates these relationships.

Quality Control of Purchased Material

This book relates to quality, quality control, and purchased material. The term purchased material, however, will be used in its broadest sense. It includes raw materials, such as steel stock or chemicals. It includes parts and assembled units often referred to as components. Sometimes these assembled units are operating units such as compressors or motors, to be installed in the final product. Purchased material, as we will use the term, also include processes. For example, a vendor may be given the task of plating material furnished by the contractor in accordance with a defined process. Services can also be purchased; a supplier may be responsible for product maintenance at a particular location, advertising services, or contracted legal services.

Software can also be purchased from a supplier. *Software* usually refers to computer programs, cards, or tapes that are used in relation to product testing or use. The term *software* may also refer to the documentation to be maintained by a supplier. Quality is important in any of these purchased materials for each can affect the quality of the overall product shipped to the customer. Any quality control program must consider the applicability of each of these to the particular product.

Previously we talked about quality and the quality program or system. This system consists of activities or tasks that must be carried out to achieve product quality. These activities and standards apply to the supplier. If the items purchased are complex, the supplier may be called a contractor. In any case, if a product is to possess quality, the many parts, materials, and processes that make up the product must be controlled. It is with these activities related to quality of purchased items that this book will be concerned.

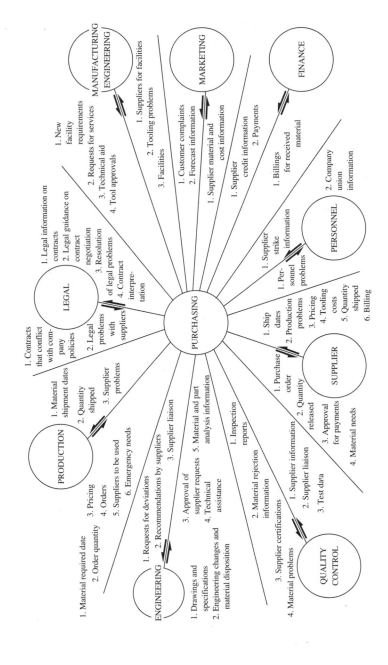

Figure 1.1   Relationship of purchasing to other functions.

Benefits to a Supplier

A quality program can be imposed on a supplier, but it is much better if the supplier recognizes the importance of quality and initiates an adequate quality program. A quality program can provide several benefits to a supplier: (1) improvement of reputation among customers, (2) reduced costs due to improved quality and reduced rework and defective material, (3) improved marketability of products due to improved quality, (4) improved employee motivation and satisfaction from doing a good job, and (5) increased sales.

When product quality is inadequate, costs increase, schedules are delayed, rework and scrap increase, deliveries are late, productivity declines, and customers are lost. When quality improves and a company has a product better than the competitors, productivity increases, employees are happier, and more customers are gained.

Why Help the Supplier?

Some managers just say certain problems are the responsibility of the supplier and question the need to help solve the supplier's problems. They may say, "It's not our problem." However, in many situations, when we help the supplier, we are helping ourselves. Without knowing the customer's forecasts for volume and schedule of a product, a supplier cannot plan to ensure our needs are met. Without fully understanding our process and the exact use of the supplier item in our product, the supplier may miss an opportunity to resolve potential problems before production starts and to give the customer exactly what is needed just when it is needed. In actuality, the supplier's problems will be our problems.

TQC and TQM

One goal of a competitive business is to provide products and services into which quality is designed, manufactured, marketed, and maintained at competitive costs. The terms *total quality control*

(TQC), *total quality management* (TQM), and *companywide quality control* (CQC) have been used to describe comprehensive company-wide systems or programs for achieving this goal. Under these systems or programs, all parts of an organization, including marketing, engineering, manufacturing, finance, purchasing, and customer service, contribute to achieving this objective. TQC or TQM have been incorporated into broad strategic plans of many of the most progressive organizations. This book defines how the supplier is an important cog in this strategy.

Part of Strategy

A firm must have a plan for dealing with both external and internal resources. Although many leading companies have always viewed product quality as an important element of their strategy, the late 1970s and early 1980s have witnessed a change in attitude toward quality by many more companies. In the past, higher-level management may have tended to view quality as a given. It was viewed as being controlled by inspection rather than as a function with goals, objectives, and measured results requiring continuous top management attention. Company goals often lacked specific quality objectives to go along with other elements of the company operating plans. The company strategy often did not include achievement of quality. To be competitive, a company's strategy must include both internal quality objectives and quality control standards as well as objectives for suppliers of materials, products, and services.

When labor was cheap, one could more readily sort bad items from good and send the bad ones back to be replaced or fixed. If the defect was not recognized and was sent on to the customer who used the product, it could be returned for repair or serviced at a user location. However, skyrocketing maintenance and repair costs—along with consumer safety regulations and costly court decisions related to product liability—have made everyone increasingly concerned with quality. It is costly for manufacturers to handle, service, repair, and return defective supplier parts. A production line shutdown for lack of parts can result in an enormous loss. Management, in turn, has become more and more concerned with quality as customers demand warranties, federal agencies require recalls, and courts give large awards resulting from defective products. Suppliers who have adjusted to these concepts have become more competitive in a market where price and delivery are not the only measurable factors.

Implementing Strategies

Establishing a strategy based on this concern can take many forms. The strategy might be included in other overall business objectives. For instance, the Motorola Company set a corporate goal to improve total quality by a factor of ten. Recognizing further the contributions suppliers make to product quality, Motorola has established a strategy that encourages suppliers to improve their performance. As another example, the Texas Instruments Corporation has developed a supplier strategy and has established a goal, to maintain supplier-quality performance, of meeting or exceeding a 98 percent lot-acceptance rate. Besides measuring the supplier's performance, Texas Instruments also measures the supplier's schedule performance by recording the number of lots received early, on time, and late. Delivery performance is measured in terms of days before or after scheduled delivery. The Texas Instruments supplier program includes these elements, which might easily be a part of anyone's program:

- Supplier conferences
- Materials/quality teams
- Audits
- Negotiating teams
- Quarterly management reviews
- Option/corporate agreements

In its supplier program, Texas Instruments has documented its strategy and developed activities associated with the strategy. The activities include supplier conferences in which the supplier is apprised of the program through a formal presentation.

Product Requirements

Chapter 2

A supplier delivers products or services to the buyer in accordance with require- ments specified in the contract or purchase order. The buyer has stated the requirements, and by agreeing to the contract, the suppli- er has agreed that it can and will comply. If the product delivered meets the requirements, the supplier has performed satisfactorily; however, if the requirements are not met, the supplier is in default. Both the supplier and the buyer want the delivered product to meet the requirements; disputes sometimes arise, however, as to whether the requirements have been met. An objective of both parties should be to specify clear and complete requirements so that a min- imum of disputes occur. Returns and repairs can be costly to both parties in terms of both money and schedule delays.

In the past, many companies worked under the assumption that engineers designed products and specified requirements, manufactur- ing built the products, and quality control inspected the product after it was made to ensure quality. Since the 1940s, the concept of quality control has gradually evolved into an emphasis on manufacturing quality products that meet the customer's requirements, with only a limited amount of inspection by quality control personnel. Quality control personnel now spend greater effort ensuring that quality is built into products and that conformance to requirements is achieved as the products are made.

The same line of reasoning can be applied to the quality relationship with a supplier. The objective is to assure that items or materials provided by a supplier conform to requirements without the need for extensive inspection upon receipt by purchaser. This chapter deals with the approaches to this quality concept and the means of its accomplishment, beginning with the careful definition and specification of requirements.

Specifications and Standards

Specifications and standards are documents containing criteria that must be met. These consist not only of physical and performance requirements but also of procedures that the supplier must perform on the equipment—such as tests, material control, and reliability verification. In dealing with suppliers, these specifications and standards become part of the purchase order or contract and become legally binding documents, as part of the contract. They define what is being purchased. Definitions of the commodities to be purchased can also be contained in engineering drawings, catalog descriptions, or other documents.

Each document must be incorporated into the purchase order so that there is no doubt that the requirements are part of the contract agreement. If a requirement is not stated in the purchase order, the purchaser has no direct basis for enforcing compliance. Many requirements are discussed in the process of source selection and negotiations; some are intentionally discarded as being unnecessary, whereas others become part of the agreed-upon standards.

Standards discussed verbally between the buyer and supplier but never placed in the contract or purchase order often become problems later. Verbal agreements may fail to reach the responsible supplier personnel, or one of the parties may not understand that they are to become part of the final contract agreement.

> **Case Example.** The requirements for on-time delivery of a critical piece of test equipment were discussed during the negotiation stage with the supplier, but a delivery clause was never placed in the purchase order. Even though the purchase order required status reports against milestones, the supplier did not start construction of the equipment until after the delivery date. As a result, the equipment was delivered a year late, and the buyer was unable to meet its delivery schedule due to an inability to test the product. Subsequently, the purchasing department initiated a policy to impose penalties for late deliveries on all contracts. The penalty clause prompted a study of delivery capability by both customer and supplier.

Clearly, all agreements must be stated in the purchase order or one of the referenced documents to be enforceable.

Conformance to Standards or Requirements

Every product has standards to which it must conform. Product characteristics, dimensions, and process requirements are established by design engineers and are placed on engineering drawings. As the products are produced, measurements are taken using a gage or other device to determine if the dimensions are within the allowable tolerance. Engineers may also specify that performance requirements be demonstrated. Requirements may state, for example, that equipment must operate under various environmental conditions, such as at a temperature of 140° C while at a reduced voltage. Product capabilities of this nature can be verified by conducting a test with the equipment operating at that temperature and under the specified load. An endurance test or a life test can also be made on a sample to verify life or reliability specified for the item. Sometimes a purchaser requires that the supplier provide products that perform in a specific application. To meet this condition, the supplier needs to know how the products will be used. In such cases, suppliers should hesitate to change a supplied product, even if it appears that the specified product requirements are not affected. Before making the change, the supplier should verify that the change will not make an impact on the customer's product or process.

Quality can be defined as conformance to the requirements, and it becomes of utmost importance to ensure this conformance. An important part of the manufacturing and quality control function is to assure that the standards and other requirements have been met. Quality control personnel either verify conformance of the product to the standards and specification requirements or ensure that conformance has been verified in the process of manufacture or testing.

Establishing controls to ensure that quality requirements are met can be broken down into steps.

1. Identify the needed characteristics and the criticality of each.
2. Select an appropriate unit of measurement, such as centimeters or volts, to define each characteristic.
3. Establish a standard value and an allowable tolerance for each value.
4. Develop a process to produce the characteristic. Design either a process-control chart or another technique for use during manufacture.
5. Choose a gage or test instrument that can measure each value.
6. Where appropriate, select sampling plans.
7. When the item has been manufactured, measure the product characteristics.
8. Determine the difference between the product value and the standard or required value.

9. Accept or reject the item based on the finding.
10. If the product is not acceptable, determine whether the defect could be a random occurrence or attributed to a cause.
11. Take action as necessary to prevent further occurrence of nonrandom defects.

The concepts of quality control do not require that every dimension or requirement be checked on every item or even on the sample inspected. In fact, it is better to carry out a task or activity (such as process control) that will assure that products are manufactured correctly to begin with. Most processes can be controlled to ensure that defective items are seldom produced. If the process-control methods are at all dubious, however, samples can be taken and measured for verification as the manufacturing process is carried out. This is much better than producing a large quantity of items and then attempting to determine what percentage are acceptable or trying to sort the good from the bad parts. With the increasing use of robotics, many processes include automatic devices to inspect every item with an automatic kick out of rejected items.

Where Are Quality Standards Defined?

For purchased commodities, all important characteristics should be specified as part of the standard purchase agreement. For example, the phrase "All hazardous materials must be marked" can be part of the boilerplate requirements on all purchase orders. Other requirements pertaining to specific commodities or to one item only can be established by the use of engineering specifications, blueprints, physical samples, catalog descriptions, commercial standards, performance specifications, material specifications, drafting standards, or workmanship standards.

In other cases a *general specification* or *supplier specification* may list requirements that apply to all procured products, such as testing a certain number of items from each lot or furnishing test data to the contractor. Sometimes quality systems specifications or inspection documents are used. Test specifications also describe how tests are to be conducted, frequency of testing, and the required documentation to be prepared from the tests. Frequently, an item is described by reference to an industry standard, as for a specific type of steel bar stock or a standard chemical. For military products, quality conformance requirements are often provided within the standard document or in referenced standards.

Engineering Drawings (Blueprints or Prints)
An engineering drawing is a pictorial and/or narrative description of an item, including dimensions and other descriptive information. The dimensions include tolerances and are given in sufficient detail to avoid possible misinterpretation. Common definitions should be used to avoid misinterpretation. If common definitions are not usable, definitions should be provided on the prints. Use of a common drafting approach (such as ANSI Y 14.5) will eliminate potential interpretation errors. It also provides definitions for terms often misused. In procurement, a company will use drawings showing the supplier exactly how the item is to look. Drawings often describe processes used in the manufacture or treatment of the item and are frequently used to depict machined parts, castings, fabricated items, forging, or other custom items.

The manufacturer must know the revisions to each standard that applies. It is common for the purchaser's inspectors to mistakenly use a different revision of a drawing than the supplier used, particularly in cases where a change was not specified in the purchase order.

When buying according to a drawing (print), the drawing number and revision (plus any applicable changes) must be specified as part of the purchase order. For example, the purchase order may state "Deliver 50 items in accordance with General Co. drawing #400654 Rev. C, and changes 1 through 6." The supplier then manufacturers the items and ensures conformance to the drawing before it ships to the purchaser. Upon receipt from the supplier, purchaser's inspection personnel can inspect the item against the same drawings, comparing dimensions and other requirements used by the supplier. If the supplier has been selected properly and the requirements stated adequately, the inspection personnel might only need to check the supplier's data and verify its adequacy, and then the material can be delivered directly to production.

When drawings are used, it is the supplier's responsibility to meet the standards, dimensions, tolerances, and other requirements given on the drawing. It is the buying company's (contractor's) responsibility to ensure that the drawings are correct and complete and that the design meets the performance and other end-use needs of the product and its users.

Physical Sample
In some cases, the product to be delivered by the supplier is defined by a physical sample furnished by the contractor. The supplier can compare products produced with this sample. Physical samples are particularly helpful in establishing limits on appearance requirements, such as paint-splatter density. With samples, less descriptive information is necessary. The physical sample is satisfactory as a standard in cases where the item to be furnished is not complicated and where material content and tolerances are not important. In production of a toy, for example, while a model may be acceptable, a purchaser may still need to write some requirements into the purchase order, such as avoidance of sharp edges, loose pieces, or toxic materials. Tolerances are less important as long as the item functions as intended.

Samples may also be used successfully in the purchase of fruits, eggs, or other items in which the quality or size can be compared to samples for grading. It would be difficult, however, for the buyer's receiving inspection department to determine whether a product is identical to a sample if inaccessible internal dimensions and tolerances, or material composition of the item are to be verified.

Samples can present problems, however, when they need to be reproduced, especially if they won't be reproduced for two or three years. First, samples may degrade with use and time. Second, maintaining physical standards over time becomes difficult due to the many variables involved. For example, paint-splatter samples depend somewhat on viscosity, humidity, and pressure—factors that are subject to change. In addition, it is not always easy to compare the product to a sample.

Brand Name or Catalog Description
Suppliers often publish catalogs in which their products are described. The catalog could contain the performance characteristics or other descriptive material. A buyer can then select the desired item based on the catalog description. The catalog could reference product warranties, interchangeability, material composition, or other standards that apply to the item. Selecting a catalog item is one of the simplest methods of specifying a product, but a number of problems are associated with this method. First, it often restricts a purchaser to a single supplier, unless the item to be purchased has an industry standard, and more than one supplier produces the same item. Furthermore, when there is only one source, the supplier is less likely to negotiate on prices or be willing to make changes or provide special characteristics needed for product applications. Also, any disruption in the supplier's production, such as a strike or quality problem, may result in manufacturing schedule delays for the purchaser.

In some cases, the item purchased by brand name or catalog description is patented, which again restricts the bidding to a single supplier. In cases in which the engineer specifies a brand name, however, the purchasing agent should exercise authority to seek an alternative product that would satisfy the need. If alternative sources are found, the bidding can be more competitive, and work disruptions or quality problems at one supplier plant will not disrupt the contractor's production.

One of the main drawbacks of ordering by brand name or catalog number is the difficulty in determining what characteristics to inspect or test at receiving inspection. The design engineer or quality engineer can, however, furnish the receiving inspection personnel with information on the important characteristics.

Problems can also arise due to the control of a proprietary design by the supplier. For example, the buying company may have been using a catalog part for a long time and found it satisfactory. The supplier, perhaps wanting to improve the product, then makes a change in the design or in a material that does not affect the catalog description. All of a sudden the using company experiences a problem. After considerable time and effort, it determines that the supplier is using a new material and that the new material becomes distorted in the user's application. The supplier had not realized that the change in design or material would affect the usability by a customer. This type of problem occurs frequently, since it is not easy for a supplier to be fully aware of all uses of each product, and sometimes a use involves unusual environments where moisture, heat, or cold are present. One way to prevent this problem when using a catalog is for the customer to create a document ensuring that the supplier notifies the buyer before making any engineering changes.

Commercial Standards
Purchasing to commercial standards provides many advantages for both the using company and the supplier. Sometimes industry standards are developed by a particular group such as the electrical industries. In other cases they are national standards. Sheet steel, screws, pipe, chemicals, lubricating oil, and many electrical parts are normally purchased according to commercial standards. When buying this way, the purchasing department can easily request competitive bids and select the supplier offering the lowest price. There is complete clarity as to exactly what is wanted and needed. A commercial standard cannot be changed by the supplier alone, and each party knows exactly what inspections or tests can be performed. Usually, the parts or materials can be obtained quickly because they are carried in a supplier's inventory.

Controlling quality on receipt of the shipment may be more difficult. The commercial standard may list some characteristics that are easily inspected, whereas others, such as strength or material content, are not easily verified. In general, however, this method of purchasing should cause the least number of quality difficulties as long as the user's application is correct.

There are some disadvantages to using commercial standards. Since the commodities are used in many applications, the purchaser's ability to define his or her special needs is limited. A special need, such as burr-free edge material, generally requires modification of the commercial standard.

> **Case Example.** A timing belt used in a complex electronics device was specified by use of a commercial standard. The electronics device experienced intermittent defects that were traced to flash on the timing belt. The flash, however, met the requirements of the commercial specification. In order to resolve this problem, the design engineer issued a special specification to require the removal of the flash before use of the timing belts. This corrected the problem.

Sometimes a commercial standard is mentioned in the supplier's catalog or on the goods themselves. An example is the abbreviation UL, meaning approved by Underwriter's Laboratory. In other cases, products will indicate conformance to certain federal agency requirements, such as those of the Food and Drug Administration (FDA). Many of these standards exist, but there is no assurance that these stipulations will satisfy a particular user's needs. It is very helpful, however, for the information to be available to persons performing inspections and tests.

Performance Specifications

A performance specification can describe what an item is required to do and under what conditions. For example, a 2 HP, 1800 RPM motor is described as being able to operate with a certain torque at -40 to $120°$ C. The supplier of the motor determines how to achieve the performance by selecting the size, weight, or type of motor. In other cases a specification describes the exact physical size and mounting and how the purchased item fits with other parts of the final product; it may also specify dimensions, weight limits, or other characteristics. The specification may also state exactly how the item is to be tested, or it may state any other method by which the performance is to be verified.

Performance specifications may be used when the purchaser lacks knowledge about the design of the part or does not care about the construction of the item and is primarily interested in its function. Such specifications are particularly useful in specifying products that perform a function, such as software. The engineer is willing to leave the design details up to the supplier, as long as the necessary functions can be performed.

The use of performance specifications gives the supplier substantial freedom in design of the item, provided the performance is achieved. The supplier will be able to take advantage of up-to-date methods or materials, or can use patented items. Therefore, the purchasing company using performance specifications may expect to obtain lower bids from suppliers than it would if the design were exactly defined. In any type of procurement, if a company is restricted to only one supplier, the company should ascertain the credibility of the supplier and should examine alternatives. Some suppliers tend to promote their more expensive products when a less expensive item would suffice. Performance specifications are also useful in establishing which characteristics are most important to a user. Aerospace companies, as one example, include a multiplication factor in their pricing considerations that recognizes weight as an important factor. In aerospace products, added weight means a loss of capacity plus more fuel.

Commodities Standards

Developing specifications for each type of commodity will result in consistent quality requirements. A typical company's commodities listing will give us an idea of the scope of these standards as follows:

adhesives
aluminum
batteries
bearings
belts
blowers
cable
capacitors
capital equipment
carbon products
castings
chemicals
clutches
coils
computer items
connectors, contacts
copper
cathode ray tube displays
crystals
electronic components
engineering supplies
fabricated parts, assemblies
fans
fibre, phenolic parts
fuses
gages
gaskets
gears
glass products
hardware
household moves
integrated circuits
lamps
lubricants, oils

machined parts
magnets
maintenance, repair
motors
nameplates
office equipment, supplies
packaging materials
paints
paper products
plastic
plumbing supplies
power supplies
printed wire boards
printing supplies
relays, solenoids
resistors
ribbon, print
rubber parts
safety equipment
service contracts
shop supplies
sleeving
sockets
software
solders
springs
stampings
steel
switches
tapes
tools
transformers
varistors
wire

Material Specifications

Companies often prepare material specifications for use in ordering from suppliers because such specifications provide control over the exact makeup of the purchased material or item. A material specification lists the composition of the desired material or otherwise describes its chemical and physical properties. Typical purchases are raw materials, lubricants, liquids, paints, or other substances. How can the material be checked upon receipt from the supplier? Normally an analysis cannot be performed to verify the composition of the material. In some cases controls are established at the supplier's facility to ascertain that the composition is sufficiently controlled during the processing. The supplier then furnishes test reports or certification of compliance.

There are advantages and disadvantages in using material specifications. When material specifications are used, the buyer assumes a greater responsibility for quality. As long as the supplier furnishes the material in accordance with specifications, the buyer must make sure that the material as described will meet the end-use needs. Moreover, the buyer who uses company material specifications may not be aware of recently developed materials that may perform equally well at a lower price or provide better performance at the same price.

Once the buyer runs a qualification test on the supplier's material, the supplier should not make changes if the purchase order calls out the material specification. In the absence of specifications in the purchase order, a supplier may make improvements in processes or designs. Since the supplier is not aware of exactly how customers use the material, the process change might result in adverse effects for a particular customer.

Workmanship Standards

The lack of workmanship standards can result in the fabrication of parts that meet the basic requirements but do not function properly, are unreliable, or have an unacceptable appearance. Workmanship standards include but are not limited to quality of solder joints, definition

of burrs, breakaway, concentricity, flatness, squareness, surface roughness, characteristics of welds, wire wraps, flash, taper, blow holes,
crazing, coloration, and appearance. The degree to which each of these
is defined depends on the product application and criticality. The
appearance of a refrigerator door may prevent its eventual sale even
though it will not affect its function. A poor solder joint or weld joint
may result in a reliability failure of an airplane or pressure vessel.
Establishing required workmanship standards before negotiation will
minimize misunderstandings and problems.

> **Case Example.** The parties discussed appearance of a unit
> during negotiation but they never documented it in a mean-
> ingful fashion. When the unit was produced, it looked good
> but was the wrong color. Further negotiation resulted in
> reworking the unit to the right general color, but it still did
> not match, since no tolerance on color had been established.
> Additional definition and more costly rework eventually
> resulted in an acceptable product. The extra cost and delay
> would have been avoided with an appropriate, documented
> workmanship standard for appearance.

Content of Specifications and Standards
While specifications used in the procurement of products or materials
usually are similar in format, the length and detail of the various parts
of the specification can vary considerably. The company acting as cus-
todian of the specification will be named on the document along with
the engineer or others responsible for its preparation and maintenance.
The responsible engineer will prepare and maintain the document in
accordance with format and change procedures established by the
company. Sometimes the supplier, if a sole source of procurement, will
be named in the specifications. In other cases alternate sources of supply may be listed. Listing suppliers in the specification gives guidance
to the purchasing agent but also limits the agent's ability to secure other
sources from which purchasers can be made. Listing the supplier's

name may also necessitate revision of the document whenever a new supplier is located or an old supplier is to be removed.

The specification will contain the product name and a specification number in accordance with the company's standard numbering procedure. The applicable revision letter and any changes incorporated will also be given on each drawing or specification. The product or material description and/or performance requirements make up a substantial part of the specification. Sometimes drawings or other process or test specifications are referenced and become part of the specification requirements. The documents may describe the performance of the product, give detailed dimensions, set power consumption requirements, set noise or environmental restrictions, establish minimum safety requirements, or specify materials to be used. In any case they must include sufficient description so that there is no question as to exactly what is to be furnished by the supplier.

Dimensions, characteristics, or defects may also be classified as to their importance. Possible defects that are life threatening, such as the release of a toxic substance, and requirements important to the functioning of the product are identified as much more serious than characteristics that affect appearance only. All these characteristics, along with tolerances, are often referred to as quality characteristics.

The specification also describes the ways in which the requirements are to be verified and establishes criteria for final acceptance. Qualification tests prove that the design of the product will perform as required. They are usually performed before many items are built. However, parts may be periodically requalified. Acceptance tests or inspections are performed on each unit or on a sample of the units from each lot. A sampling plan may be included as part of the specification.

Finally, the specification will contain information as to how the item is to be packaged along with any prescribed methods of handling, shipping, or storage. It may also include requirements for labeling, restrictions on storage life, or other storage conditions allowed or not allowed. Labeling requirements may specify bar coding for certain information such as part numbers and supplier code numbers as included in the Automotive Industry Action Group (AIAG) specification E-3. By using bar-coding tables, computer-aided bar code readers can assist with stocking or shipping activities. Operating and maintenance procedures are usually given in other documents, such as handbooks.

Environmental Requirements

Products are used under varied conditions. A part used in a freezer needs a different set of standards than a part used in a washing machine or an airplane. Extreme temperature, pressure, humidity, and shock are examples of use conditions. The conditions under which the performance and other standards must be met are often called the environmental requirements. Before deciding that a part furnished by a supplier will perform in the necessary environment, the engineer will review the catalog information prepared by the supplier or confer with the supplier about the needed performance. At some point the engineer will want to see test results proving that the part will perform as claimed and may decide that special tests are to be performed. These tests, called *qualification tests*, include testing under the specified environmental conditions. When the tests are completed satisfactorily, the item is considered *qualified*. The purchasing agent must make sure that supplied items have been qualified before placing orders for production quantities. Storage and shipping conditions must be considered part of the use environment of the product. Sometimes warehouse storage temperatures or temperatures encountered in transportation can be exceedingly hot or cold.

Specifications: Pros and Cons

The use of specifications has several advantages to the company buying the purchased items or materials. First, the engineer has to carefully think through the exact needs and the requirements to be specified. If this is done well, it removes or reduces the likelihood of future misunderstandings due to lack of clarity or inadequate definition of dimensions, standards, or other specified requirements. A company will usually want two or more suppliers of the same item. The use of a detailed specification will help ensure that items obtained from any of the sources will be identical and interchangeable. However, care must be taken to ensure that process variations do not affect the interchangeability. For example, a rolled thread and cut thread may meet the same specifications but perform differently.

When a specification is used in procurement, it is easier to secure competitive bids from several potential suppliers. Both the bidders and the contracting company can be sure that each supplier is bidding on the same thing. Each supplier knows exactly what is needed and can be assured that every other bidder is pricing the identical item. The increased competition in the bidding process is likely to result in a lower price and in less risk of the product failing to meet requirements.

When the completed product is eventually received by the receiving inspection department, the specifications and drawings can be used to verify that all standards are—or are not—met. The supplier's quality control personnel will have had the same documents to work with, a fact that should reduce the possibilities of disagreement on whether requirements are met.

Engineers, however, sometimes have a difficult time describing all the conditions important to a part or product. The U.S. government tries to solve this problem by a flow down of specifications (i.e., each standard or specification listed in a standard is also considered to "flow down" as a requirement). This flow continues until no additional requirements are listed. Still, a specification for a complex item may reference as many as three to four thousand standards. In this process of using the flow down, the specifications may include conflicts. If they do, and the conflict is not recognized beforehand, a difficulty may arise in meeting a requirement, possibly resulting in a waiver.

As an alternative, some supplier-customer relationships operate on a commitment from both to achieve the desired results. To accomplish this, the customer explains the application of the supplier's part in the customer's product. The impact of defects are explained and demonstrated so the supplier understands the process needed to make the part fit the customer's needs. Both evaluate the part to assure that it meets the characteristics in the specification and the intended use. Process capability values are set, evaluated, and calculated for critical characteristics. Trial parts are constructed and critically evaluated throughout assembly. Once the required characteristics are demonstrated, the supplier and customer agree that if the basic part criteria change, the customer pays for the change; if the part changes and is wrong, the supplier takes the responsibility. The supplier also has the responsibility to correct a process causing a problem even though the specification may allow the condition that caused the supplied part not to work.

Product-Use Information

By human nature, a person who understands how a particular item is to be used and why certain requirements are important will probably exert more care in the job. Experience has also shown that educating workers about the product, process, and customers results in improvements in workmanship and quality. Showing workers how defects affect the product and customer helps the workers take responsibility for their actions. This concept needs to be extended to supplier's personnel. Some companies send out teams to the supplier plant to survey the plant and to inform its personnel about the problems that exist when specified requirements are not being met. Similarly, if a supplier's manufacturing personnel visit the contractor's plant and see exactly how the supplier items are used, perhaps they will better understand and accept the actual need for each specified requirement. Otherwise, they may see the requirements only as an abstract group of standards.

From a higher-management point of view, if the manager of the supplier's plant came into the user's plant and saw a production line shutdown because of defective parts, the importance of each standard might be better appreciated and the problem would receive greater attention.

There is, of course, another side to the product-use information coin. Sometimes a contractor will specify tolerances tighter than actually necessary. If the supplier's personnel find this to be true on some occasions, it may result in careless treatment of all requirements, to the detriment of both supplier and contractor. Working closely with a supplier in the early stages of a contract can help a contractor eliminate unneeded requirements and reduce costs. If the supplier is invited to submit suggestions during the original bidding or negotiation, a more satisfactory product description can be arrived at. Suppliers often hesitate to make suggestions during the original bidding or negotiations for fear of being judged noncompliant or incapable of meeting the specified requirements. This is, however, the best time to identify unnecessarily stringent requirements and arrive at standards that will meet the needs of the final product and also be within the capability of the supplier's manufacturing facility.

A supplier also has some implied legal and moral responsibility to provide goods suitable to the purpose for which they are to be used. This is particularly true when the final product is a commercial item such as a washing machine, iron, etc. This responsibility may even extend beyond the exact standards specified. If the supplier has not, however, been advised of the end use, and the items later turn out to be unsuitable for the intended use, the purchasing company has no recourse against the supplier except to claim that the product should have worked.

> **Case Example.** A supplier was providing a part to an original equipment manufacturer (OEM). A detailed product specification was issued that described the product characteristics and how to evaluate each characteristic. Engineering limit samples were used for characteristics difficult to place in specification format. As a result of advances in computer technology, the OEM began to use the product in an application that it had not previously conceived but that was within the potential use of the product.

The product did not perform for one characteristic in the new application. The supplier stated that its product had not changed and met the engineering specification. Evaluation of the product by the customer demonstrated that the current product matched the engineering samples, and the characteristic was well within engineering requirements. This evaluation included measurement of over one thousand pieces with each measurement taking one-half hour. During the evaluation, the customer also determined that 90 percent of the products would give the end user a problem in the new application. The OEM requested the supplier to repair products held in the warehouse and stop product shipment until the problem could be designed out of the product. Repair of the products in the warehouse would have cost about $40,000 (two thousand hours at $20 per item).

After several supplier-customer meetings at various levels of management, the supplier agreed to make and pay for the repairs. The logic used by the supplier was that even though the product met all engineering requirements, the customer could not use the product. The customer was able to demonstrate that competitive supplier's products worked as expected in the new application. Going to court would not have been the best choice for either.

A fully informed supplier will probably go out of the way to help the customer. If a potential supplier does make suggestions for revised requirements, and the ideas are accepted by the buying company, the specification or purchase order must incorporate the changes. This, however, still does not relieve the purchasing company of responsibility in the event of future problems related to the suggestion. Neither can a purchasing agent just leave it up to the supplier to furnish a usable product. The purchasing agent still has the primary responsibility to management and will be held responsible in case problems occur later. Therefore, the purchasing agent should take the lead in providing an atmosphere for cooperation between supplier and contractor throughout the procurement process.

Validity of Standards

A standard that is too lax may result in a product that will not perform as needed. It could also cause the product to lack sufficient life or reliability or to fail to work correctly with other parts in the finished product. Incorrect tolerances, for example, may result in items that do not fit together properly with other parts.

Standards that are too stringent may cause costs to be greater than necessary, possibly resulting in a product not competitive in price. Higher prices of supplied items, because of unnecessarily stringent standards, can result in reduced company profits.

Standards must be valid—that is, neither too lax nor too stringent. Validity can be affected by inaccuracy or incompleteness of the requirements; lack of clarity; omission of recent design changes; failure to use up-to-date materials, parts, or processes; or omission of applicable customer requirements. It is also important to avoid inconsistent standards, incomplete descriptions, and ambiguous statements. Furthermore, it is important to define the method of verifying each requirement. The test equipment and testing sequence used by the supplier should not damage the product and should be compatible with that used by the contractor. This necessity of compatibility also applies to calibration, gages, other methods of measurement, and conditions under which tests are conducted. Problems in any of these factors can result in a lack of valid standards. Regarding evaluation, however, keep in mind that inspection after the fact is a poor replacement for process control. Requirements should be stated in a fashion that they can be maintained and verified throughout each step of the process.

Clear Communication of Requirements

Standards involve interpretation. Many quality problems arise between suppliers and contractors because the supplier interprets a standard differently from the contractor. The following illustrate some communication problems.

Terms and Definitions

Terms such as *smooth surface* or *no scratches* are insufficient as quality standards. While a hairline scratch may be acceptable, there is probably some depth at which the scratch becomes unacceptable. A degree of surface smoothness acceptable for some applications may be unacceptable for others. Where these or similar terms are used, an agreement must be reached as to the exact definition. These definitions, when agreed upon, should then be documented as part of the design drawings or specifications and thus become part of the purchase order.

Judgments and Tolerances

Tolerances on dimensions are usually easy to define, since they are measurable. Nevertheless, care must be taken to properly show the dimension on the engineering drawing. Dimensions from points on imaginary surfaces to centerlines of holes are difficult to measure without special instrumentation that may not be available. In cases involving characteristics such as color, roughness, or purity of a liquid, less precision is possible, and it becomes more difficult to have a clear standard. Samples or pictures may be helpful to clarify the criteria, but both supplier and contractor must use identical samples when they perform their inspection. Sometimes it is useful to prepare physical models showing acceptable and unacceptable conditions. Unusual curves and shapes are often difficult to describe in words, so use of identical, duplicate models by the supplier and contractor can reduce the number of cases in which the supplier judges the item to be acceptable while the contractor rejects it. Developing standards showing the extremes of all acceptable conditions is difficult, since the extremes of individual items may be acceptable but the extremes of all combinations are not.

Maintaining the revision level of these standards and producing an item exactly like the standards each time are not easy tasks. Each revision requires a plan for production and verification. Furthermore, wear on a tool master requires the tool to be recertified by the supplier and/or purchaser to ensure it still conforms to standards. Remaking a tool master is also a challenge, since it needs to be the same as all other masters.

Of course, both the supplier and the contractor are interested in avoiding conflicts or differences of opinion. Even though one of the parties may win out in a particular disagreement, any controversy is costly to both parties in terms of time, money, and trust. The supplier has the natural desire to satisfy the customer. However, there is a limit to what can be done in order to provide this satisfaction. On items already shipped or manufactured, any changes or remaking can be costly. Both supplier and contractor have profit as one of their management objectives.

Many companies have standard manufacturing practices, workmanship standards, design standards, or lists of standard parts for their product, but the standards of a supplier and the contractor would not normally be identical. If, in the negotiating phase of a contract, the supplier and the contractor exchange copies of their standards, each can review the other's for differences and potential problems. A supplier normally sells to many customers, and each customer might have a set of standards, sometimes with differing requirements. It may be difficult for the supplier to meet the diverse needs of several customers. However, this interchange of information with each customer early in the negotiating phase will help both the supplier and the contractor. Whereas minor differences might easily be resolved, some serious differences may suggest the selection of a different supplier. Some companies also have quality control practices or procedures. Exchanging information on these standards early in the negotiating stage is also helpful in avoiding problems later.

Procurement of Services
Establishing requirements in the procurement of services is just as important as in the purchase of goods, but the need is not always as apparent to the buyer.

Services can be grouped into three categories: (1) *technical services*, such as software development, service manuals, or maintenance, (2) *professional services*, such as engineering, legal, or consulting services, and (3) *operating services*, such as food service, janitorial service, or grounds maintenance. For any of these types of services, many firms use a *statement of work*, which defines the work to be accomplished, preferably in terms of the result desired. Since quality has been defined as conformance to requirements—or conformance to customer needs—a means is needed to measure how well the service has been accomplished. When feasible, the fee paid for the service can depend on the degree of conformance to the requirements or objectives.

Standards, Practices, and Policy

Some companies take the view that standards, including tolerances, should be somewhat tighter than actually necessary for product functions or performance. This practice can tend to become a company philosophy of tolerances tighter than necessary, but loosely enforced. This concept rarely provides productive results for either the company or its suppliers. Experience has shown that in the long run it is better to specify realistic standards and tolerances and enforce them rigidly. In later chapters of this book, we will deal with acceptable deviations from requirements. However, this should not suggest that a company establish the practice of relaxing requirements, nor of accepting out-of-tolerance items on a regular basis. The best policy is to set standards that are needed, can be met by the supplier, can be verified, are not meant to be relaxed, and are enforced except in unusual circumstances. If an out-of-tolerance item is accepted, a plan of corrective action should be taken to prevent further occurrence. However, if an out-of-tolerance condition can be accepted with no effect on performance, reliability, or appearance, a specification revision should be made.

Specification Review

A specification contains the detailed requirements that a product must meet. From the viewpoint of the purchasing department, there are two categories of specifications. In one case the entire specification describes a product to be procured from a supplier. In the second case the product described by the specification is to be manufactured in-house, but some of the materials and parts called out in the specification are to be procured from suppliers. The specification review applies to both situations. It is a systematic procedure in which various functional groups of the company—such as production, tooling, manufacturing, engineering, quality control, testing, and purchasing—examine the specifications, usually prior to formal issuance. Quality control personnel demand clarity of requirements and the ability to make checks and tests of the dimensions, tolerances, and other characteristics. The purchasing representative checks for available sources of supply, necessary lead time, and price. Suggestions for alternative materials and parts are important contributions of the buyer.

Where purchased parts and materials are involved, it is usually necessary for purchasing to make contacts with potential suppliers in order to secure answers to important questions. Are the items readily available, or will they have to be specially made? Are tolerances realistic? The questions asked should address both quality and economic considerations. Potential suppliers are often asked to look over a specification to help answer these questions. Any agreed-upon changes can then be incorporated prior to the signing of the subcontract agreement.

Change Control

The control of design changes is sometimes called *configuration management*. The word *configuration* refers to an item and the particular drawings or specification changes that apply. An item made according to revision A would be of a different configuration than one made according to revision B, even though most people could not readily see a difference. Likewise, an item made according to revision B and change No. 1 would be different still. The term *configuration management* refers to a systematic set of procedures for identification, control, and accounting for the design changes. The objective is to make sure that the correct changes are reflected in each piece of equipment and to have records to show which changes are incorporated into any particular equipment. The concept of configuration management originated in defense procurement and applies mainly to complex equipment. An individual product may be subjected to a configuration audit to ascertain exactly which design changes have been incorporated into it.

Change control applies to all procured items. It is important to know exactly which drawing changes have been incorporated in any item. The purchasing agent has an important role in the change-control procedure and in making it work so that the configuration of any item can be determined. The purchase order should specify any relevant revision.

Change control is crucial for inventory control. Revisions fall into several categories. A *class 1 change* is one that affects form, fit, or function; generally such changes require a part-number change to maintain control as well as to mark a clear *break-in* point. The cost of a class 1 change is generally high, since spare parts, maintenance manuals, and peripheral activities are affected significantly. *Class 2 changes* do not affect form, fit, or function and, therefore, do not require as much control. The best control, however, would be to keep records to show where each change is incorporated.

Quality Control Responsibilities for Specifications

Engineering personnel are generally responsible for the preparation and content of specifications. This does not mean that quality control personnel or suppliers have unimportant responsibilities, however. The best procedure is to allow quality control people and suppliers to review supplier specifications when they are initially prepared and also when any revision or change is proposed. The quality control or test personnel can often make suggestions related to the following:

1. More effective test methods
2. Sampling plan usage
3. Difficulties in checking certain characteristics with available gauges
4. Newest measuring techniques

5. Clarification of requirements where there might be more than one interpretation.
6. Requirements or dimensions where no method of verification is given
7. Tolerances difficult to meet on existing manufacturing equipment
8. Clarification of the relative importance of requirements, or the degree of verification needed for each requirement

Identification and resolution of any of these potential problems in the review can prevent later problems with the supplier.

Responsibilities of the Purchasing Agent for Quality

A purchasing agent is responsible for all aspects of a procurement—including schedule, cost, and quality of the material procured. When a specification is given to a supplier for bidding purposes or as part of a subcontract, the supplier often has questions on interpretation. Suppliers may also make suggestions for changes in the specification. The purchasing agent acts as a go-between for the supplier and the engineer who prepared the specification. It is usually not sufficient to pass along the questions and the answers. Where something can be interpreted in more than one way, the purchasing agent should demand that the specification be changed so that it can be interpreted in only one way. As an alternative, clarification can be added to the purchase order. If a change is to be made in specifications of an existing subcontract, all bidders, or multiple suppliers, should have a chance to see the change and comment on the possible effects. Problems of delivery, cost, quality, fit, or performance could result if changes are not given to all affected suppliers for review prior to actual implementation.

Quality Requirements vs. Type of Contract

Various types of contracts and their effects on quality and quality control are discussed in a later chapter. Here, however, it is appropriate to mention that there is a relationship between the type of contract and the firmness of the quality requirements. With the firm fixed-price contract, the supplier bids on exact requirements, expecting little variance from these requirements in later negotiation, unless a party suggests an improvement or a change needed to correct a deficiency in the product.

In other cases, both the supplier and the contractor recognize that the specification requirements are subject to change, possibly because the product is in the development stage, or for other reasons. As a result, the buyer may utilize either a fixed-price redeterminable contract or a cost reimbursement contract, either of which would allow the supplier to be reimbursed for the cost of any changes. These two types of contracts are recognized as being more likely to undergo requirement, schedule, and price changes subsequent to their signing. A change in quality requirements could result in a schedule change and/or price adjustment.

Negotiating Quality Requirements with a Supplier

In some procurements, the specifications and requirements are sent out to potential suppliers for bids. When the successful bidder has been identified, some matters must still be negotiated before it can be said that the subcontractor has been firmly selected. In other procurements one supplier may be selected for negotiation without going through the bidding process. The negotiation phase provides an opportunity for the contractor and the supplier to carefully go over all the terms of the specifications, drawings, and other documents included in the purchase order.

One objective is to assure a common understanding of the standards and requirements, including quality requirements. Whenever any dual interpretations arise, there is an opportunity to make the clarification and place the clear definition in the contractual documents. Suggestions by either party for doing something in a less expensive way or in a manner that will improve performance, product life, or reliability can also be considered in the negotiation process. The bargaining on the quality aspects is done concurrently with bargaining on schedule, price, and other factors over which opinions differ. These factors are not independent, since changes in quality standards may affect price or delivery dates. The interrelationships are not always obvious, however, and a considerable amount of judgment and intuition is involved. In the negotiation process, some quality characteristics will be flexible, whereas others will have little or no room for change—depending on their relationship to product function, reliability, safety, and so on.

Some people view the negotiations as an exchange in which the buyer is trying to get the price down and the seller trying to get it higher. In reality, it is not so simple. All factors—including schedule, price, and quality—interrelate and must be considered together. Bidding on standard items involves the least negotiation; procurement of one-of-a-kind items involve the most.

Prior to entering into negotiation with a supplier, a purchasing agent will usually develop a strategy for the company. Engineering, quality, and scheduling personnel should all be involved in the process. All of them, however, need not always be present in the meeting with the supplier's negotiating team. Having the quality expert on call is often an effective way of proceeding. The negotiating strength of the buyer will depend on several factors. Is there more than one available supplier? Has the buyer implied that a contractual arrangement already exists with another supplier? The purchasing agent who has developed alternate suppliers and has laid out strategy is in a better position to negotiate favorably for the company.

Those involved in the negotiation should carefully prepare for it. The quality and purchasing people should be familiar with the specifications, the items being procured, and their use in the final product, even though most technical questions will be directed toward the engineer. Without knowledge of the more important and less important characteristics, the quality representative will have difficulty responding to suggestions or requested changes from the supplier's negotiating team. There should always be a designated leader of the negotiating team to assure the presentation of a unified position on each item negotiated.

In preparing for the negotiations, specific objectives should be established. Objectives like "getting all we can" are of little value. Setting limits on price and schedule and identification of critical quality characteristics are more valuable. In some cases the customer organization is so large that poor communication may exist between engineering, quality control, and purchasing staffs. When this happens, a supplier must work with three or more customer organizations. Moreover, the supplier may hear three or more different stories and must obtain a resolution.

Summary of Purchasing Strategy to Achieve Requirements

Strategy is an overall plan by a company to achieve its objectives. We have stated that the purchasing agent is responsible for quality, schedule, and price. The purchasing department has a number of ways to achieve these objectives:

1. Use multiple sources or provide for alternative sources so that the company does not become dependent upon one source of supply. Obtain competitive bids or price quotations.

2. Concentrate on fewer suppliers, but take steps to assure they will be long-term, quality suppliers.

3. Before placing orders, evaluate sources of supply based on past performance and capabilities observed during visits to the supplier facility.

4. Define all the essential or helpful information carefully in each subcontract and purchase order so that the supplier fully comprehends the requirements and is given the clear responsibility to meet them.

5. Withhold payments to suppliers until there is reasonable assurance that products received meet the requirements.

6. Evaluate the received material as soon as possible after receipt. Make acceptance conditional if certain requirements cannot be verified at that time.

7. Require the supplier to furnish evidence with the material showing that the requirements have been met. This evidence could be test or inspection reports.

8. Visit the supplier's facility to inspect or verify the status of material prior to shipments.

9. Establish good working relationships with suppliers.

10. Educate the supplier on the requirements and why they are important in the use of the end product.

11. Research the financial stability of each potential supplier.

12. Define procedures in the subcontract for handling design changes without excessive costs or delays.

13. Provide technical assistance to suppliers when they request assistance or do not have the capability to solve their quality problems.

14. Research the supplier's stability by studying any changes in management, reductions in force, organizational structure, factory cleanliness, orderliness of material, and personnel attitude.

15. Determine if the company has been certified to ISO 9000 (discussed in Chapter 4).

The Price of Quality

Chapter 3

In his book *Out of the Crisis*, Dr. W. Edwards Deming, world-renowned consultant, states that improvement of quality transfers waste of worker hours and machine time into the manufacture of good product and better service. As early as 1949, management in some Japanese companies observed that improvement of quality results in improvement of productivity. Once Japanese management adopted the chain-reaction concept illustrated in Figure 3.1, quality became the aim.

The key ideas here are that

1. improving quality, in the long run, saves money rather than costing more, and
2. improving quality is the most cost-effective route to higher productivity.

These ideas are critical in developing a supplier-customer relationship and strategy.

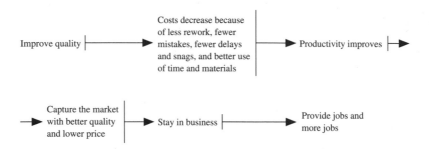

Figure 3.1   The Deming chain reaction.

Quality Costs

Some firms limit the cost of quality to the costs of inspection and test. In the past, this has often resulted in noncompetitive products. Any successful quality strategy must consider the cost of product nonconformance as compared to the cost of conformance. Payments for rework, calling products back from the user, and other costs of nonconformance are all factors to be recognized.

Each department in an organization must be able to justify itself by measuring its costs and comparing those costs with the department's contributions to company objectives and profits. Quality control must be included in this equation. Thus, it becomes important to determine an overall cost of quality.

Importance of Quality Costs
For a company to decide if the price of achieving quality is worthwhile, it must consider the price it would pay for not having quality (i.e. the cost of poor quality). The cost of poor quality today accounts for a growing proportion of a company's total costs. This expense falls heavily upon a manufacturer or service organization; the cost of poor quality may amount to a large percent of the sales billed. This not only affects the costs billed by a supplier to the customer; it also increases costs endured by the customer as failures occur in the factory or later, after the product is shipped to the final user. One important factor in a

supplier-customer relationship is to be able to measure these costs and eliminate their causes. This chapter will discuss ways to do this. The buying company and the supplier should each have systems for measuring the costs of quality, including the costs of poor quality, which are preferably part of their normal accounting systems. Ideally, the supplier's and buyer's systems would be compatible. The next question, then, is how the supplier can use this information generated by the accounting system.

Cost of Quality Defined

Some people break the *cost of quality* (COQ) into four components:

1. Prevention costs—costs incurred to prevent defects in the products
2. Evaluation costs—costs incurred in determining that products comply with requirements
3. Internal failure costs—costs incurred when products are found in the factory that do not meet requirements
4. External failure costs—costs resulting from defects found after the product leaves the factory

The two failure costs are the same as the costs of poor quality, but they can also include costs related to liability when users file lawsuits due to product failures.

These costs are further defined as follows:

1. *Prevention costs*—costs associated with planning and carrying out the quality program tasks that take place before the product is manufactured. The following are examples of tasks that can be classified as prevention costs:
   a. Design review
   b. Employee training and certification programs
   c. Supplier evaluation before awarding subcontracts
   d. Quality control engineering, including design of special tooling and equipment

  e. Process controls to assure that manufacturing processes hold product tolerances

2. *Evaluation (or Appraisal) Costs*—costs associated with measuring conformance of products to standards, including inspection and tests. The following are examples of tasks associated with evaluation costs:

  a. Inspection and testing of incoming parts and materials from suppliers

  b. Inspection and testing of materials, parts, subassemblies, or completed products manufactured in the plant

  c. Cost of products destroyed or damaged by destructive or life tests

  d. Calibration and maintenance of inspection gages and test equipment

  e. Quality data collection, records, and reports

3. *Internal Failure Costs*—costs that occur prior to shipment (or while the producing company still owns the product). These costs result from defective products (products failing to meet requirements). The cost of the following fall into this category:

  a. Value of products scrapped

  b. Rework costs to make defective items conform to standards

  c. Cost associated with analysis of failures or defects to determine cause

  d. Cost of reinspection or retest of products that have been reworked

  e. Reduced value of products sold as seconds due to defects

4. *External Failure Costs*—failures that take place after the customer assumes ownership of a product contribute to this

category of costs. These costs include the following through the period of warranty:

    a. Replacement of defectives

    b. Repair costs

    c. Costs of receiving and processing complaints

    d. Liability of producer due to product hazards, usually incurred through liability insurance costs or litigation

    e. Loss of future orders or damage to reputation due to defectives received by customers

An alternative definition, which breaks the COQ into two components, is gaining widespread use.

COQ = Price of Conformance + Price of Nonconformance

The *price of conformance* (POC) represents the price of all activities and materials aimed at getting the job done right the first time. These can be called the *good* dollars. The following fall under this category:

Quality education	Inspection and testing
Training	Quality planning
Design reviews	Quality systems and
Design verification	procedures
Process controls	Quality audits
Process verification	Salary of quality manager
Preventive maintenance	and staff
Inspection and test planning	Supplier surveys

These, again, are the costs related to getting things done right the first time.

The *price of nonconformance* (PONC) represents the price of all efforts and materials expended when things are not done right the first time. These costs are often associated with the product; however, hidden labor and systems costs should be included.

These wasted costs fall into the following categories:

Scrapped products	Downtime
Rework or reprocessing	Overtime to meet schedules
Material review	Returned material
Troubleshooting and retesting	Warranty costs
	Hidden costs of lost sales
Failure analysis of both factory and field failures	Product-liability suits
	Excessive inventories
Salaries of customer service people handling complaints	Paperwork relating to any of the above
	Telephone calls relating to any of the above
Unscheduled service	

You might ask why the term *price* is used instead of *cost* in this case. We do so to highlight the point that management has a choice—just like a consumer chooses the price she or he wants to pay. Management can choose to pay the price of conformance rather than endure the price related to nonconformance. CEOs have learned that doing things right the first time, though not always easy to get underway, saves in the end.

Note that the PONC includes some items that managers often consider part of the normal costs of doing business. These include service organizations to handle customer complaints, material review boards to handle disposition of nonconforming items, staff to determine the status of late shipments and late receipts from suppliers, costs of administering problems related to warranty programs, inventories to compensate for defective items, spare parts for failures, production downtime due to delayed parts, redoing a purchase order, and others. They also include costs for finding materials ordered late, lost orders, missing forms, and premium freight or overnight mail resulting from not doing something right the first time.

Accounting System
The finance and/or accounting departments in a firm must permit or force managers to pay close attention to financial data. Financial

statements and budgets provide the tools to communicate any problems. These financial data work best when they show managers a dollar measure of nonconformance in their department so that each manager can take corrective action.

Past data have shown that the price of nonconformance in some manufacturing companies runs as high as 20 percent of sales dollars, and this percentage is often higher in some service organizations. Thus, presenting nonconformance costs in each manager's financial statement can present an opportunity for substantial dollar savings. A statement showing income can show income reducing items right alongside. These include costs such as returns, warranty costs, sales concessions on seconds, lost discounts when bills are not paid on time, special delivery costs, and similar items. Alongside operating expenses, the statement can list nonconformance costs such as rework, scrapped parts, reprocessing, replacement parts, and so forth. Each manager should have the responsibility to take corrective action for these costs, just as the manager would be expected to take action for any budget overrun under her or his responsibility and control.

When this nonconformance information appears in the regular accounting reports of a supplier, it benefits both the supplier CEO and the customer who audits the supplier quality. In evaluating potential suppliers, a buyer can ascertain that the supplier has a method to control the cost of poor quality, which also means that overall supplier quality will be better. The supplier CEO will be able to see the actual cost of not doing things right the first time and the impact on the company's cost of doing business as well as the product quality. Many organizations are using this method to improve the quality of their product or service while reducing costs at the same time. Earlier in the chapter we said that improved quality saves money. The presentation of nonconformance-cost information in the normal accounting system integrates quality improvement into the regular budgeting and cost-control system, which can make a significant contribution to a supplier's competitive position and profitability. When the supplier CEO recognizes this, the job of the quality auditor becomes much easier.

Supplier Costs

Unless supplier costs are properly assessed, the full impact of supplier's material on the user's facility cannot be determined. The measure of this impact can be achieved by determining the value of total cost of goods sold as compared to the value of supplier material received. The higher this ratio, the greater the supplier's impact on the user's business. While the source of these costs was defined earlier, some further aspects should be considered.

Incoming evaluation has become increasingly costly and often exceedingly difficult. Complex material and parts require high expenditures for test equipment to evaluate complex systems. For some electronic components, equipment to perform evaluative tests at receiving inspection can cost hundreds of thousands of dollars. Equipment for measuring mechanical characteristics of piece parts in general is also very expensive, difficult to obtain, and not thorough in assuring that all dimensional characteristics meet requirements.

In assessing the need for inspectors, the user should consider the number of parts received versus the number of lots received. If sampling inspection is used, inspection cost is related to the number of lots. In fact, during periods of low business, the level of incoming inspection personnel may not reduce significantly, since only lot sizes might be reduced. If the number of lots is also reduced, incoming inspection personnel reductions can be considered. In the case where all parts are inspected, the cost of inspection personnel is directly related to production needs and the amount of material being received.

In any case, many users are choosing to use the supplier documentation and test verification data to demonstrate that each unit meets contract requirements and performance specifications. High inspection costs also explain why managers are moving toward programs that place more responsibility on suppliers to provide 100 percent acceptable products. Good quality products received by the user's facility can be placed directly into stock or can be placed directly at the production line for immediate use.

If confidence in a supplier is not achieved, the user's overall inventories increase due to delays at receiving inspection. The JIT concept reduces these inventory costs, since supplier goods can be placed immediately at the production site. It is advantageous for the user to be able to depend on the supplier's quality system, since in-process checks can be performed by the supplier but are not available to the user. If this objective can be achieved, it will result in reduced expenditures by the user for equipment necessary to assess product conformance.

Program Assessment

When establishing supplier costs, the user must determine what factors to use to evaluate the effectiveness of the supplier's quality program. Once established, these factors should be budgeted and monitored to assure that conditions do not get out of control. Increases of inspection costs per lot received or per piece received can be indications of poor quality performance by the supplier. Levels of charges for scrap and rework are an indication of supplier problems also. The gathering and display of this information can be used as evidence to encourage improved vendor quality. Regardless of the action taken, without the data being displayed and presented to management, a supplier quality program will have little positive direction or aim. Management—and the supplier—will pay more attention when all the costs related to non-conformance are brought into focus.

Auditing for Quality

We see above a number of things a buyer can look for in auditing a supplier. Let's cite a few things that can be observed and would detract from a supplier's overall rating.

1. Supplier sees COQ as a responsibility within the quality control department.
2. Supplier sees COQ only as it relates to product hardware and the functional parts of the organization producing the product.

3. Rather than seeing a nonconformity as something detracting from company profits, supplier sees it as something to argue about and to try and fix fault.
4. When asked about cost of quality, supplier's people think in terms of their regular cost-reduction activities.
5. Higher-level managers, including the CEO, do not see COQ as something they work with personally.
6. Cost data are presented in categories too broad to be useful.
7. Accounting department is not part of overall quality system.
8. Financial reports are presented in terms that are not meaningful to various departments.
9. Supplier assumes that a report alone is enough to provide quality.

Some Trade-Off Concepts

The COQ can be portrayed as a trade-off as illustrated by Figure 3.2. The direct COQs include prevention and evaluation. As these costs are reduced, the number of defectives increases. As the defect level increases, the failure costs increase.

The total costs are the sum of direct costs and failure costs. At the lowest point in the total cost curve, the optimum mixture of effort is indicated. More and more firms are deciding that their optimum total cost point is at a very low level of defectives, possibly close to zero, as in Figure 3.3. This conclusion follows from several factors.

1. The high cost of lost sales due to perceived low quality by customers
2. High labor costs related to return/repair of failed products after shipment to customer
3. Feasibility of in-process controls based on automated equipment and statistical controls, jointly resulting in close to zero defectives

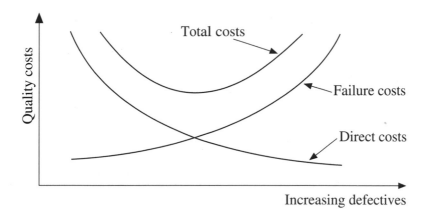

Figure 3.2   Quality cost trade-offs.

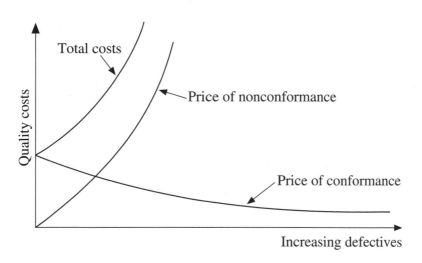

Figure 3.3   Optimum cost close to zero defects.

Supplier Quality Costs

The supplier's quality strategy must be based on COQ versus the cost of not having quality and the impact on the firm's business. Determining the cost traceable to the supplier's quality program and quality deficiencies is not always easy. The elements could include the following:

- Total value of material received compared with total inventory
- Cost of extra inventory due to anticipated problems
- Cost of extra inventory due to nonconforming material held for disposition
- Cost of rework due to supplier's defective material
- Cost of scrap due to supplier's nonconforming material

The costs related to supplier's quality and the cost of not having quality can then be measured to see their impact on the firm's profit.

The Manager's Responsibility

Three important factors enter into any COQ program.

1. Get attention for quality problems by citing cost.
2. Take corrective action to reduce cost.
3. Measure the improvement.

Reporting costs of nonconformances in the regular accounting system provides a basis for a successful program. Continuous improvement is the key, but it must gain management's attention just like other cost and expense deviations. COQ should be reported in monthly operations reports and discussed at high-level staff meetings, and its improvement should be clearly recognized and supported by the CEO as a necessity in all parts of the organization. Once established as part of the routine each month, this becomes a way of doing business.

Supplier Evaluation and Selection

Chapter 4

A primary means of obtaining purchased materials with the right quality involves selecting a supplier that has the capability to do the job. Capability includes the supplier's processes and equipment, technology, capacity, and desire to take on the necessary responsibilities.

Processes and equipment—having the processes and equipment to perform all the steps and/or having subcontractors who do.

Technology—having expertise in the product design and process development pertinent to the product. The supplier must have competent people who know the ins and outs of every process, understand the workings of the product, and have experience designing and producing reliable products in a cost-effective manner.

Capacity—a demonstrated ability to produce at the required quantity and to handle emergency and add-on orders.

Desire—a commitment from supplier's management to take on the contract responsibilities.

Furthermore, for the purchase to be satisfactory, a supplier must be capable of meeting the quality requirements and willing to reach agreement on price and schedule. These things cannot happen without careful planning and the exercise of professional skills. Sometimes a purchaser must select the best supplier from among several capable prospects. In other situations, source selection becomes a matter of finding one capable source who can meet the requirements. In still other cases, a capable source cannot be located, and the purchaser must develop one with the assistance of engineering and quality control.

Steps in Source Selection

The first step in source selection is identifying possible suppliers, sometimes called the *bid base*. For some procurements, the purchasing department will be aware of possible suppliers. In other cases, involving a product or material not previously purchased, the purchaser doesn't know who makes the item.

When no supplier is found, the question becomes "Who might be able to make the item?" Searching through catalogs, trade journals, or directories may be the starting point. Data from catalogs or qualified parts lists can help determine whether a particular supplier can meet the requirements.

The second step in supplier selection is to evaluate the possible sources and identify those who are capable and acceptable. Capability requires adequate facilities, technical know-how, and competence to achieve quality. Acceptability relates to financial stability, production and engineering competence, interest in doing business, managerial competence, and willingness to cooperate. Experience of a supplier is an important element affecting quality. Purchasers must also consider quality capabilities. For example, the resources needed to produce a few quality items in a job shop are different from the resources necessary to produce quality under higher rates of production. In the evaluation phase, the purchaser compares the relative qualifications of suppliers and the advantages and disadvantages of each. It is often desirable to select two or three sources to reduce risks and to help ensure future price competition.

Although the purchasing agent or buyer might rely to a great extent on the quality control department to evaluate the quality competence of a supplier, the buyer cannot completely delegate this responsibility. Purchasing has the records on suppliers' past performance, transmits all documents to the supplier, and is the official communication channel with the supplier. We might say, then, that the purchasing agent or buyer is the person primarily responsible for cost, delivery, quality, and the success of the supplier. The agent must fully understand the impact of subtle process and product differences when evaluating multiple suppliers. Each supplier's process is different, and parts may react differently.

Alternative Suppliers

Frequently an engineer designs a product using an available part from a particular supplier. This is often necessary to find something that will perform as required and will meet the environmental and use conditions. In this case, when the buyer receives the bill of materials, it will list the part, showing the particular manufacturer and perhaps the catalog number. Although it may be the purchasing department's policy to avoid the use of single sources, the buyer in this situation will probably have no immediate alternative to the single source. Even if the material list specifies "or equal," the buyer may have difficulty ascertaining what will actually be of equal performance and quality.

The proper procedure in this case is for the buyer to seek one or more alternative items and have these suppliers submit performance characteristics or test data for the design engineer to evaluate. If any of the alternative products prove to be satisfactory, they can be added to the bill of materials. This will allow the buyer to obtain competitive bids, and also to have backups in case one supplier is unable to deliver on schedule due to a strike, a quality problem is encountered, or other problems occur with one supplier. In some situations, the buyer may purchase from two or more sources on a continuing basis, which assures that more than one supplier is always geared up to furnish the item.

When parts or materials from two or more sources are used as equals, it is necessary to ensure their *interchangeability*, which means that either part can be used in the final product without noticeable difference in performance or need for adjustment. To ascertain this, it may be necessary to determine the variability of particular characteristics. Two brands of resistors, for example, may have the same mean resistance and be built to the same tolerances, but the distribution of one may be skewed. If the final product were adjusted to the skewed distribution, the other brand might not perform as well in the product. These types of variability problems can also result from temperature or humidity variations under use. Although two parts may appear to be identical, they might not be truly interchangeable for a particular use.

Limited Number of Suppliers

In the early 1980s many companies recognized the advantages of limiting the number of suppliers. The basic idea was that if a supplier knows that it will have business over an extended number of years—as long as it maintains quality—it will plan accordingly and be willing to spend more to develop and provide long-term quality at lower costs. General Motors refers to this concept of developing long-term agreements as life-cycle procurement.

Companies using this approach realize that suppliers who can produce good-quality items require a great deal of personal attention but are worth the effort. If a supplier is willing to make the needed investment to improve processes and productivity, lower costs and improved quality will result. The concept takes advantage of supplier know-how and talent. Many companies enter into long-term contracts with suppliers. Prior to the 1960s a one-year contract with a supplier was considered to be long-term. Today contracts up to five years are becoming common practice. A Ford executive estimated that between 15 and 20 percent of the dollar value of his company's purchases were under contracts for three or more years.

The result of this trend is for a company to rely on fewer suppliers and, sometimes, a single source for a particular part. In the past, committing to a sole-source supplier was often considered a mistake. However, this concept of fewer suppliers allows the company to allocate resources more carefully and to concentrate on those suppliers who are more promising. Materials management and part ordering become much simpler with fewer suppliers. Management policy may even exert pressure to reduce the number of suppliers. Aggressive targets of 50 to 75 percent reduction set a challenge to the organization.

> **Case Example.** A purchasing organization using two thousand suppliers was having difficulty consistently receiving material on time with the required quality. Overtime was being used to reschedule receipt of material and production. Delivery to customers was being affected by the rescheduling. The purchasing, engineering, and quality organizations were challenged to reduce the supplier base. The first step involved deleting suppliers who had a poor quality or delivery performance. If the supplier did not meet a set minimum level, no additional orders were issued. For some of the worst suppliers, delivery or quality reasons were used to cancel existing orders. This phase took three months and yielded a 27 percent supplier-base reduction.
>
> The next step was to request multiple-parts suppliers to quote cost reductions. Those that did not respond were dropped. This yielded a 8.5 percent reduction of the supplier base and a reduction in purchase price of 2 percent. At the same time, engineering evaluated similar parts and made design changes to eliminate one or more of the parts. Then purchasing had the suppliers rebid. This resulted in a 7 percent supplier-base reduction and a 5 percent cost savings for

the parts requoted. After eight months a 42.5 percent reduction in number of suppliers was achieved with a favorable purchase price variance. These changes were accompanied by improved quality and deliveries and by reduced average time to award a purchase order.

Supplier Evaluation

The evaluation of a supplier can be divided into two parts. One is the product evaluation, and the other is the evaluation of the supplier's ability.

Product evaluation involves determining whether the supplier's product is able to meet the design requirements specified—unless, of course, it is a new product, yet to be developed. In this phase, the purchaser may review test data from the supplier to see whether the product qualifies and meets all standards. Sometimes, one or more parts will be ordered from potential suppliers so that the buyer's engineering department or quality department can actually run its own qualification tests. These may include reliability, life, and environmental tests.

The second part of the evaluation is to determine whether the supplier can deliver goods that will conform to all requirements over the span of the contract. In other words, is the supplier able to manufacture conforming products in production quantities? While this phase of the evaluation is more difficult, past experience is one measure of this ability. An evaluation of the supplier's procedures, policies, facilities, and people is necessary to determine the supplier's ability to supply quality products.

Fixed-Price or Cost-Plus Contracts
In a fixed-price contract, the supplier agrees to furnish specified items, materials, or services at a set price. This is the preferred arrangement from a quality point of view whenever the requirements are definite.

A cost-plus contract provides that the supplier furnish items or services at cost, plus a fee (or profit). This type of arrangement is used in the following situations:

- The item furnished cannot be easily defined—since perhaps it is still under development.
- The supplier has never made the item, and it is difficult to determine price.
- Design changes are expected as the work progresses.
- The buyer is not willing to wait until definite requirements are available.
- Services are being procured, and they are on an as-required basis.

The cost-plus contract has risks in that the supplier has less incentive to control costs, the requirements are not as well-defined, and thus the items furnished may not meet the customer's needs.

Intracompany Purchases

Often one division of a company manufactures a product that uses a part or component manufactured by another division of the same company. Many manufacturers tend to treat these other divisions differently from other suppliers. Bids from the other divisions are not considered in competition with other suppliers on a price, delivery, and quality basis. Less formal communication methods are often used. Moreover, evaluation for process capability and capacity may not occur, and incoming inspection or defect reporting may be different. Requirements to purchase from intracompany suppliers, however, can also bring with them systems to control those suppliers.

Some companies have policies dictating the use of products produced in-house, whereas others allow free competition between internal and external sources. Past experience has shown that a restrictive policy does not work very well. When people know that they definitely have the order, they exhibit less concern for quality and schedule. The policy that treats intracompany purchases the same as external suppliers seems to provide the best overall results.

Quality Information Package

Before a buyer can evaluate a potential supplier effectively, the buyer must make the supplier aware of the requirements expected. Part of any survey or evaluation will include questioning the supplier, since it is necessary to assure that the supplier understands the quality standards and feels capable of meeting them. Remember, however, that an evaluation is usually performed with a particular procurement in mind. The fact that a supplier produces good quality on certain products is not adequate evidence in itself that quality will exist in another product. Capability *and* familiarity with the particular product is essential.

At minimum, the following are required in the information package furnished to potential suppliers:

1. Drawings and specifications
2. Descriptions of inspections and tests to be performed by supplier, including qualification tests
3. List of data and reports required from the supplier
4. Delivery schedule
5. Requirements for product identification, packaging, etc.
6. General conditions on the standard purchase order form to be part of the contract
7. Quality requirements

The intent is to inform the supplier of exactly what is needed. The supplier should examine the quality document and become familiar with it.

Existing Data Sources

Any company has many suppliers, and any supplier sells to many companies. Furthermore, qualification and environmental tests are expensive and time-consuming. The cost of testing is especially high if several items are to be tested for each requirement and if the item is destroyed in the testing process or no longer can be used as a salable product. If each company had to evaluate each supplier, there might be considerable duplication of effort, even though each company would be concerned with testing specific applications of the product. To some extent, then, it becomes economically feasible to pool data and share the results among users of a product. Sometimes a survey of a facility is carried out so that this information can be made available along with the test data. Data pools take on any number of forms.

1. *Pooled information for a particular industry.* Companies in a similar industry often have similar evaluation needs and requirements. An example is the Coordinating Aerospace Supplier Evaluation (CASE), which receives and compiles data on relevant products. The data can then be sorted by supplier, process, or product line. Member companies have agreed to furnish backup information on request from other companies. Besides providing a cost saving to purchasing companies, CASE saves time in source selection. The service is also advantageous to suppliers who now have published data available on their products and capabilities.

2. *Government programs.* The Government Industry Data Exchange Program (GIDEP) was developed to compile data on new parts and components. The primary objectives were economy and the availability of information to users.

3. *Company programs.* Many large companies have programs for companywide compilation of supplier data. These data can refer to testing, surveys, or experience. The information is made available to all divisions in the company.

Any of these joint efforts can be of considerable value when a supplier is being considered or evaluated for its ability to meet requirements. These types of efforts are usually worthwhile as long as the data are kept current, and the system contains the test data for the specific environment indicated. Problems sometimes occur if there has been a design change in an item and the test data are not current. A supplier can usually tell prospective users where test data for the supplier's products are available.

Through the use of ISO 9000, members of the European market have established a common quality system standard. Although certification to ISO 9000, as discussed in detail later in the chapter, is expensive, the benefits may out weigh the costs. The process of becoming approved results in an improved quality system. Being certified also means that a company meets the complete requirements of some customers, and it can, thus, result in more business. The use of Underwriter's Laboratories and Canadian Standard provide evaluation of common critical characteristics.

Quality in a Supplier

A supplier should exhibit an understanding of quality and its benefits and should comprehend that an effective quality program provides benefits in terms of both inputs and outputs. On the output side we see better quality products with fewer defects discovered by the user. This can be translated into repeat sales and positive word-of-mouth comments, both of which result in greater sales. In terms of inputs, defective products at any stage of production call forth increased human resources, increases in materials used, greater use of energy, tied-up facilities, and attention by management. On the other hand, the by-products of high quality are better employee morale and reduced turnover of personnel.

Much can be learned about suppliers by the way they view quality within their own organizations. When evaluating a supplier's concept of quality, note the following:

- Does the business have a quality policy, and if so, is the policy communicated and implemented continuously?
- Does each manager see quality as part of his or her responsibilities?
- Do performance appraisals consider quality as an element of every manager's performance?

- Do company personnel consider quality to be the sole responsibility of the quality control department, or does each person see quality as part of his or her own task?
- Are product problems covered up, or are they brought out in the open for resolution? Is there emphasis on blame for problems, or is the emphasis on cooperation to alleviate the problem?
- Is the company inspection oriented, or is the emphasis on prevention of defectives?
- Do quality control personnel have the power to make decisions when there is an impact on product quality?

A company with a successful quality program should take a total approach to quality as part of its overall company strategy. This means that top managers place no less emphasis on quality than they place on cost and schedule.

As Japanese companies open new plants in the United States, we notice close attention to selection of employees. These firms seek intelligent people who are reasonably well-trained with respect to their specific jobs. In addition, management seems more willing to delegate responsibility for quality of work to the worker and is willing to provide product use, cost, and other information to the employee as it relates to the particular job. Further, it seeks employees who have an attitude of cooperation and team spirit. These are factors we should observe when evaluating a supplier.

Quality Problems in Supplier Companies
In evaluating suppliers with quality problems, findings show a tendency for the different functions within a company to be working independently. One function—such as production planning, marketing, or even quality control—proceeds with its own immediate objectives without consideration of other or overall needs, such as quality. Moreover, some organizations do not encourage their employees to solve problems. Most employees do not understand the processes, and if they do, they aren't allowed to circumvent them.

Organizations sometimes view quality as either an unknown or an uncertainty. Rather than planning for quality, people wait to be told what to do. In come companies, for example, an imbalance exists between product technology and production technology. New and stringent requirements appear in product designs without the equivalent advances in production technology. Manufacturing engineers are faced with the necessity of making tooling and equipment work at or beyond their tolerance capability. It is important, then, to look at the supplier's total process and apply the proper controls to assure that the item is made right the first time.

In other problem companies, information flow is not synchronized with the flow of material. For example, drawing revisions are not released in time for use in procurement or manufacturing. This requires people to work with marked-up documents or under the threat of further changes. When the concept of quality is raised, the supplier's people tend to focus on manufacturing defects. Companies with better quality records think of quality in broader terms. Companies with less satisfactory quality records often focus on acceptable quality levels rather than on an attitude that any defect should be prevented. Furthermore, if a defect occurs, the root cause should be determined and corrective action taken.

Does the Supplier Use Any of These?

Quality control programs use various techniques. Since you may encounter these techniques in a supplier evaluation, some of the more well-known and frequently used ones are explained briefly. Complete chapters—or complete books in some cases—have been written on these topics. The objective here, however, is to provide an overview of each topic sufficient for a buyer to do his or her job. Checklist questions are also included, along with favored responses.

Quality Plans
Some companies require that prospective or current suppliers prepare a plan defining exactly how quality is to be assured. Caterpillar

Tractor Company, for example, provides a guideline for preparation of the plan by the supplier. The plan must identify control points throughout the supplier's operation, from receiving through shipping to the customer, including the following:

1. major characteristics checked, and where in the operation they are checked
2. frequency of checking
3. method used in checking
4. part of organization (i.e., quality control, manufacturing, etc.) responsible for making the check
5. records maintained, retention period, and traceability method

The plans are signed by the supplier's management people responsible for the operation and are submitted to Caterpillar's management for approval.

Quality Circles

Quality circles are small groups of employees who meet on a regular basis. Their primary task is to identify problems, analyze them, and propose solutions. The concept began in Japan and is directed largely toward quality problems—however, a wide variety of problems can affect quality. An important by-product of a quality circle is to improve communications between employees in different functional areas (such as engineering and manufacturing), and between employees and management.

Responses to the following questions will help buyers judge the effectiveness of the supplier's use of quality circles.

1. Does management support the idea and nurture the concept?
2. Is participation voluntary?
3. Do circle members select their own problems? (The answer should be yes—one purpose of a quality circle is to identify new problems.)
4. Have members been given the broad company objectives so that their actions support these objectives?

5. With what frequency do they meet? (Weekly is typical.)
6. Are monetary awards given? (Preferably not—the most effective circles are based on satisfaction gained in participating.)
7. How are problems handled when the circle identifies them? (Are documented results available?)
8. Are managerial people aware of results?
9. Do supervisors support quality circles?

Design Quality Index

Manufacturing engineers and quality engineers often review designs to determine potential difficulties in manufacture or control of quality. At that time alternative designs can be rated with a design quality index (DQI), and one or more demerits are assigned to each difficulty. Such systems can steer a company away from choosing a design with an unfavorable index.

Reliability of Design

Reliability is a measure of the product's ability to perform in the intended manner over the period of its expected useful life. Techniques are available for calculating the expected reliability of a design before the product is produced. This calculation is helpful in selecting the better of alternate designs. It also is useful in identifying potential product problems so that changes are made in the design. The calculation can then be compared to the measured reliability of the product in use. If there is a difference, evaluations should be made to ascertain the causes of the difference. For any type of product, a supplier should be able to demonstrate a knowledge of reliability, of how it applies to the product, and of efforts carried out to improve reliability in the product.

Design Review

When the engineering department has completed the drawings and specifications for a product, a design review is conducted. Engineering, quality control, production, procurement, tool design, and possibly other functions participate in the design review. The design is scrutinized, and its manufacturability assessed. Preliminary plans for tooling, routing, process controls, and inspection gauging are also established. Where solutions to problems are feasible or improvements for producibility are apparent, changes can be made in the design before the final drawings are released.

The following are examples of questions that would be raised in the design review to alleviate later problems:

1. What long lead material is required?
2. Can existing machines hold the tolerances specified?
3. Are unproven processes called for?
4. Do the processes exist to produce the item?
5. Is more than one supplier available for the purchased item or material?
6. Have life, reliability, and environmental qualification tests been performed?

After this review, the following steps can be taken to control quality in production:

1. Design or procurement of inspection gages
2. Design or procurement of test equipment
3. Preparation of process controls
4. Preparation of acceptance sampling plans
5. Initiation of life, reliability, or environmental tests to qualify product
6. Establishment of procedures for control of quality
7. Evaluation of suppliers
8. Life test and performance test on engineering sample

Production Samples—First-Piece Inspection

Obviously, determining the adequacy of tooling made for a supplied item is best accomplished by checking items made with the tooling. Initial items are often made with model shop tooling, and it is important to check the production tooling before the product goes into full production. Moreover, it is important to check any other item if there is any change in the tooling. In some cases the contractor will want the supplier to define the process controls used to ensure quality once production gets under way. Using the pilot-run method is helpful in proving out parts on an actual-case basis. These pilot runs use samples in a real assembly environment to determine what problems exist.

Quality Audit
Financial audits are commonly utilized by company managements and accounting firms to ascertain how closely accounting procedures and practices are being followed. A quality audit is similar in intent. It is performed to determine if a company adheres to procedures that can affect quality. Also, product conformance audits check a product prior to shipment, after normal acceptance tests and inspections are complete. It is not uncommon to find quality audits used to check all aspects of quality in a company. The objectives are to identify product inadequacies, nonconformances to procedures, or inadequacies in existing tests or inspections.

Buyers should do a quality audit of potential suppliers. Any company, however, should also audit its own quality system. A supplier who shows evidence of auditing its own quality system can be expected to have a more mature quality control operation. Results of the supplier's own quality audits could be used as a basis for information needed by the survey team.

Audits done in times of stress often have negative results for both the customer and supplier. The audit should be performed from a positive standpoint—never to prove why a problem exists. Audits performed from a positive standpoint and at times of no stress are most meaningful. A supplier should be given the opportunity to identify its own problems and establish action for improvement.

Inspection Instructions
While the blueprints or specifications define dimensions and other requirements, it is not always easy for the inspector or machinist to

determine how to perform the inspection. Just as a manufacturing engineer may define how to make the item, the method of checking can be provided on an inspection instruction sheet. This defines the characteristics to be checked and the way it is to be done. It is especially important that the primary contractor and the supplier personnel check for the same thing in the same way. Sometimes the instruction will designate characteristics to be 100 percent inspected; in other cases a sampling procedure may be designated. In most instances, however, the number of items to check on a sample will depend on quality history for the particular dimensions or characteristics.

Zero Defects

The zero-defects approach grew out of the defense and space programs in the early 1960s.[1] Asking for zero defects is another way of saying "do it right the first time." In a true zero-defects program, no level of mistakes is considered acceptable. The program involves all people in an organization at all levels and emphasizes the unacceptability of defects of any nature. With respect to a customer-supplier relationship, it involves doing exactly what was agreed exactly when it was agreed to be done. It means clear requirements, training, a positive attitude, and a plan.

When evaluating a supplier who claims to have a zero-defects program, determine whether the term is being used without the right program. Some companies wrongly use the term as a motivational concept, whereas others actually, wrongly, believe that some level of nonconformity is acceptable. If the wrong understanding is ingrained in suppliers, people may exhibit fear when a problem arises and this may be hard to correct.

Classification of Characteristics

A typical item purchased from a supplier may have a great number of requirements. For example, each screw may have a required diameter, length, thread size, head dimension, material, and plating.

1. Philip B. Crosby, *Let's Talk Quality* (New York: McGraw-Hill, 1989), 9, 65.

Clearly, each characteristic of each item cannot be checked at incoming inspection. The objective of a classification-of-characteristics system is to provide guidance to inspection or test personnel as to the importance of the various characteristics. This does not imply in any way, however, that less important characteristics are not a concern.

Some tolerances may affect safety, reliability, performance, or fit, whereas others may be specified by customary or standard tolerance priorities. It seems logical, then, that the frequency of checking could vary depending on the importance of a requirement. The controls built into a process would also affect the degree of checking required. Classification of characteristics is normally done during design and might appear on the drawing or other document. A supplier may also offer suggestions as to what characteristics are more important in an item.

Classification of characteristics should be set by individuals in engineering, quality control, and procurement who have experience with the part. The selection helps the supplier to set priorities for process control and assures that the supplier is placing emphasis on the characteristics that most affect performance. But, everyone involved in contracting must understand that when classification of characteristics is used, a low classification does not excuse nonconformance.

Parts Per Million

In past years many companies established an acceptable quality level (AQL) of one to five percent. This meant that the targeted defect level could be one to five percent in a lot of material. Recently, in recognizing that defect levels of that order of magnitude are completely unacceptable in international competition, many firms have specified defects in terms of parts per million (PPM). A figure of one hundred PPM would be lower than a one percent AQL by a factor of one hundred. One of the main objectives is to be able to eliminate piece-by-piece inspections, or even sampling at incoming inspections. In evaluating a supplier, finding that PPM is used provides assurance that the supplier is in tune with some of the latest quality control ideas. AQLs do have a niche in production and management processes, however, if they are used with a complete understanding of the risks.

Supplier-Rating Systems

Some contractors employ a supplier-rating system that gives a quantitative rating to each supplier. The rating is usually based on results of past shipments, in terms of acceptance or rejection. The usefulness of a rating system depends on what goes into the rating figures and simplicity of use. While a rating might be useful in highlighting better or worse suppliers, it alone is insufficient to determine acceptability.

Some supplier-rating systems use only the results of acceptance or rejections at receiving inspections. They would then neglect latent defects found later in production or after the final product leaves the contractor's plant. Even if the system takes into account the seriousness of defects found, investigation is necessary to determine (1) which of the supplier's products has been rejected, (2) whether corrective action has been taken since, and (3) whether new products will introduce new problems. The general concept of a supplier-rating system is to attempt to measure ability of a supplier to control quality and service. Some systems establish a rating by combining delivery performance with failures that accrue during use.

Supplier Surveys

An evaluation or survey before a contract is signed does not ensure that a supplier will comply with all requirements, but it will certainly help to indicate those suppliers who cannot or will not comply. In general, supplier surveys identify suppliers who are not capable of delivering a quality product. Most surveys are ineffective in determining the ability of a supplier to produce consistent quality products.

Perhaps a survey prior to part production should only be used to indicate capability, technology, and capacity. It would be more appropriate, then, to say that a survey can help to ascertain those suppliers who may be able to comply.

A survey cannot evaluate all aspects of a supplier's potential performance. The main purpose is to seek out the facts and use them in making judgments as to the ability and desire of the supplier to fulfill the quality requirement. In some cases a problem or failure to perform results from a condition not evaluated in the survey. In other cases a problem derives from the purchasing company. But it is not the customer's responsibility to ensure product quality. A supplier has the ultimate responsibility. If the supplier cannot meet the requirements, the order should not be accepted.

A survey team should examine the supplier's entire quality system by checking *where quality is controlled* throughout the supplier's plant and *what control technique is used* at each point. Some methods are discussed in this chapter, while others related to inspection and testing are covered later. In addition, ascertaining the adequacy of equipment used to perform the check is very important. One purpose of the survey team is to document a benchmark of the supplier's quality program. The follow-up survey then will indicate any changes. If a different person performs the survey, it becomes difficult to compare results.

Preparation for a Supplier Survey

Prior to conducting a supplier survey or visiting a supplier facility, the evaluators should undertake considerable preparation. First, they should become familiar with the drawings and specifications for the items to be procured. Knowledge of tolerances is important to evaluate the capabilities of the supplier's machines and equipment. Cleanliness requirements may make a special clean room necessary. Environmental requirements may require special testing chambers. Personnel with special assembly skills may also be important. A checklist is very helpful in determining what is to be observed in the survey and in recording the findings.

Often it is important that inspection equipment at the supplier's facility be compatible with the purchaser's equipment. In other cases the supplier may need certain equipment, since the purchaser does not have it. The team should also be prepared to explain to the supplier how the part is used and the importance of the part. This explanation gives the supplier an additional viewpoint.

Outside Evaluation Services
Bringing quality control personnel to a supplier's plant can be expensive, especially when distances are great. If several companies are being evaluated as potential suppliers for one order, the costs can be prohibitive. One alternative is for a purchasing agent to contract with an outside professional service. Such companies employ quality control professionals who can handle quality control tasks. This is also an alternative for contractors who do not have their own professional staffs to perform surveys themselves. A company that uses an outside service should fully educate the person who will be performing the survey. A good source of outside service personnel is retired people from the customer's business.

Compatibility of Measuring Equipment
Many quality problems result from nonagreement between test or inspection equipment at different locations. The differences can be in equipment calibration or precision, in the methods used when conducting the measurements, or in interpretations of standards. Differences between factory and field equipment often occur, as do differences between purchaser's and supplier's equipment. It is not uncommon for the purchaser's inspection personnel to reject material, only to have the supplier reinspect it, find it acceptable, and return it—only to have it rejected again. In the final analysis, the supplier is not always wrong.

As part of an initial supplier evaluation, any potential inconsistencies should be identified and corrected. Plans must be made for periodic correlation checks to avoid any variations from the original standards. Locating and correcting these deficiencies in compatibility may seem costly, but later losses in time and dollars can be much more costly. The best choice is for the supplier to evaluate the product in process to ensure 100 percent conformance. When a supplier demonstrates this capability, receiving inspection is not necessary.

Checklist for Supplier Survey

When conducting a quality survey of a supplier's or potential supplier's facility, it is easy to come into a situation where the supplier shows only what is wanted to be seen. The good points would, of course, be emphasized. A checklist allows a company to evaluate on a consistent basis. It also provides a set of questions for the supplier. The objective of the survey is to determine if the company being evaluated is doing the right things to achieve quality. It also attempts to determine if these things are being done in the right way.

The checklist includes a place to rate each item. The person or persons conducting the survey should attempt to evaluate the supplier more from evidence as to what is done than from what the supplier may say is done. For example, the surveyor must verify the statement that design reviews are conducted. Written minutes of design reviews showing action items could be considered verification. On the checklist in Figure 4.1, many items to be rated are accompanied by examples of evidence that can be requested. In some cases, the surveyor can take a copy of the evidence back to the plant for further evaluation or future reference. The ratings are qualitative, so the persons doing the survey must be competent in the many quality control areas and able to evaluate each item as it is discussed.

The following rating system can be used with the checklist:

Outstanding: The supplier is judged to have a very effective system. (This rating would be rarely used.)
Good: The supplier's system appears to give very acceptable results.
Average: The methods and activities observed meet minimum standards in most cases, but some improvements are appropriate.

Inadequate: Activities are not adequate to provide quality, or the function is not performed at all by the supplier.

An alternate measure could be considered as follows: Award either a 1 or a 0 to indicate whether a characteristic exists. Here are some examples:

	Value	
	NO	YES
—Does the procedure exist?	0	1
—Does the procedure include requirements?	0	1
—Is the procedure being followed?	0	1
—Is there action to achieve conformance for rejections?	0	1

By using this latter method along with Figure 4.1, a numerical value can be obtained.

A business can also use the Malcolm Baldrige National Quality Award guidelines as a measure of the supplier's quality characteristics and performance. Whatever the instrument, however, if a company's management measures itself and acts on its findings, improvement can be achieved.

ISO 9000

The ISO 9000 series of international standards establishes quality-systems management requirements for use in contracting. When one or more of the standards are required in a contract, the supplier must demonstrate its capacity to meet the standard through audits. Every department of the organization is affected. The standards consist of five sections:

ISO 9000—A guideline for selection and use of the ISO standards. Clause 8.2 of the standard provides a guideline for determining which standards apply to a particular business.

Company Quality Policy	Outstanding	Satisfactory	Average	Inadequate
1. Is there a quality control policy? (copies of policies, procedures, or manual, copy of table of contents of manual.)				
2. Are policies or procedures updated periodically?				
3. Are policies meaningful and appropriate? (Are responsibilities clearly defined in the manual?)				
4. Is there a procedures manual? Is the manual used? (Look for copies in use and revisions.)				
5. Are operators responsible for controlling quality characteristics they produce?				

6. Is production measured for quality conformance?

7. Does top management support quality? (Talk with top-level managers; obtain views of quality control personnel and operators.)

8. Do other departments respect the quality department?

9. Is the quality control budget adequate?

10. Are there reports of overall quality and quality costs? (Ask for copies of the reports; who sees and uses them?)

Figure 4.1   Checklist for Supplier Survey.

Supplier Personnel and Organization	Outstanding	Satisfactory	Average	Inadequate
1. Is there a company quality policy and definition of responsibility? Are managers competent?				
2. Is the quality control (QC) organization well defined? (Assess chart.)				
3. Where is QC placed in the overall organization? (Assess chart.) Who does QC manager report to?				
4. Are QC engineering personnel adequate? (Talk to QC engineers and inspectors.)				
5. Are QC supervisors on an adequate level?				

6. Are inspection personnel competent? (Talk to them.)

7. Obtain evidence of personnel training. (Course outlines; talk to inspectors and others.)

8. Are personnel motivated? Talk to:
   a. inspectors
   b. shop personnel
   c. shop supervisors

9. Are procedures complied with?

Figure 4.1 (Continued)

Supplier QC in Purchasing	Outstanding	Satisfactory	Average	Inadequate
1. Does purchasing accept responsibility for price, quality, and delivery? Is one of these given greater emphasis than another?				
2. Do quality personnel review purchase orders before bids are obtained? (Talk to purchasing agent and engineer.)				
3. Do engineers and QC personnel participate in supplier selection?				
4. Is there a system for rating vendors? (Obtain a copy.)				
5. How are engineering and quality requirements communicated to vendors? (Obtain examples.) How are changes to requirements controlled?				

6. Is receiving inspection area adequate? (Visit area.)

7. Are requirements specified to receiving inspection personnel?

8. Are rejected lots identified and segregated?

9. Are shipments awaiting inspection held in an enclosed area? (Inspect area.)

10. Is purchasing notified of lot rejections?

11. Are lots inspected before supplier is paid?

12. Are quality characteristics identified for inspectors?

13. Is sampling used and understood by the inspectors?

Figure 4.1 (Continued)

Supplier QC in Manufacturing	Outstanding	Satisfactory	Average	Inadequate
1. Are design reviews used?				
2. Do operators have means of checking their work? (Observe operators.)				
3. Is inspection adequate? (Are defects found later?)				
4. Are gage calibrations current? Are calibration procedures adequate? Is a history maintained for each gage?				
5. Are drawings available to operators and inspectors? Is there a system to ensure changes are available?				

6. Are defective items identified to prevent use? Are records maintained of defectives produced?				
7. Are process-control charts used?				
8. Is there a system for quality improvement?				
9. Is a quality audit used? What actions are taken on problems found in the audit?				

Figure 4.1 (Continued)

Finished Products	Outstanding	Satisfactory	Average	Inadequate
1. Does QC participate in packing, storage, and shipping?				
2. Is there a system for handling customer complaints?				

Facilities	Outstanding	Satisfactory	Average	Inadequate
1. Are facilities adequate?				
2. Is there a calibration lab?				
3. Are inspection areas clearly designated?				
4. Are production and test areas in good order?				

Figure 4.1 (Continued)

ISO 9001—Quality assurance system for a business having responsibility for design/development, production, installation, and servicing.

ISO 9002—Quality assurance system for a business having responsibility for production and installation.

ISO 9003—Quality assurance system for a business having responsibility for final inspection and testing.

ISO 9004—Guidelines for a quality assurance system. This standard provides general guidelines for quality system elements and quality management.

Throughout the standards, the word *supplier* refers to the company that is being certified. It does not refer to the suppliers of that company. The standards for 9001, 9002, and 9003 differ from each other primarily in two ways: First, the scope of the business determines which standards apply, and second, some requirements are less stringent than others. ISO 9000 provides an annex entitled "Cross-Reference List of Quality System Elements." This cross-reference provides a summary of the paragraphs that apply to a particular standard (i.e., 9001, 9002, or 9003).

Other documents closely match these ISO standards. These include ANSI/ASQC Q90, Q91, Q92, Q93, and Q94. In addition, EN29000 and BS 5750 closely relate to the ISO standards.

When to Use ISO 9000

Each business must make its own decision about becoming certified to ISO 9000. Customer requirements and management objectives are the primary factors in reaching this decision. Some customers specify certification to ISO 9000 as part of the contract requirements. If it is specified in the contract, the decision becomes whether to retain the customer imposing the requirement or convince the customer to delete ISO 9000 from the contract. Some companies choose to become certified to ISO 9000 in order to improve their marketing position. Regardless of the reason, becoming and staying certified requires planning, dedication, and follow-up.

Sections in the Standard
The standard contains the following types of requirements. Some apply to all three of the standards (9001, 9002, and 9003), whereas others apply to only one or two as indicated below.

Management Responsibility
(applies to 9001, 9002, and 9003)
The business must identify those responsible for the quality system and the level of authority of each. This requirement applies to persons responsible for control, maintenance of corrective action, verification of activities, and management review.

Quality System (applies to 9001, 9002, and 9003)
The business must have a defined and documented quality system defining the necessary actions to meet the customer requirements. Although each business sets its own format, the system as documented must enable audits to be conducted so that the customer can confirm the adequacy of the system and the documentation. This usually takes the form of a quality manual and implementing instructions.

Contract Review (applies to 9001 and 9002)
The business must have a method for reviewing and checking contracts. These reviews should identify customer requirements and determine if the requirements can be met and the delivery dates achieved. Product, logistic, and quality control specifications should be included in the review, and appropriate records should be maintained to show the results of the review.

Design Control (applies to 9001 only)
A documented method is needed to verify that the product design meets specified requirements. The business must demonstrate design and development planning, assign responsibilities to qualified staff, define organizational and technical interfaces, define and design input requirements,

document that design output matches design input requirements, and verify design conformance and control of design changes.

Document Control (applies to all three standards, but 9003 is less stringent than 9002)
The business should have a defined method to control all specifications, standards, or legislative documents. This should include provisions for review, issue, and control of every document. Basically, the intent is to ensure that documented procedures are current and that the latest version is used at every location. This procedure must include a method for recall or destruction of superseded documents.

Purchasing (applies to 9001 and 9002)
The customer's product and system requirements must be reflected in contract or supplier documentation and evidence must prove that the contractor or supplier meets the criteria. Adequate records are needed of subcontractor or supplier acceptability and ongoing performance. A method is required to ensure that no ambiguity can occur when an order is placed. A method is also required for changes in purchase orders and other supplier-requirements documents.

Customer-Supplied Material (applies to 9001 and 9002)
The business should have a method for clearly identifying customer-supplied material and assuring that it is not included in another customer's product. The procedure must ensure that the material or equipment is adequately protected and that if any damage occurs, the customer is to be notified.

Product Identification and Traceability
(applies to 9001, 9002, and 9003)
A method is required for product identification and traceability to insure that the identification can be maintained. Although the method will most likely vary based on the nature of the product, the method and procedure for identification and traceability must be implemented so as to meet customer and legislative requirements.

Process Control (applies to 9001 and 9002)
The business should have a documented method for planning and implementing written instructions for the manufacture of the product to meet the customer's requirements. The documented method and written instructions should include product specifications and the defined responsibilities and instructions, particularly if their absence would adversely affect the quality of the product. Particular attention should be given to documented process requirements where no quality control checks can be made to determine conformity to the specification after manufacture.

Inspection, Measuring, and Test Equipment
(applies to 9001, 9002, and 9003)
The business must have a documented system that defines the control in a calibration program of all equipment used to measure the conformity of products. The system should include (1) the method for identifying equipment to be calibrated, (2) the system to ensure that equipment is calibrated at defined intervals, (3) the method for recording the traceability of calibration to national standards, (4) a system for checking test results of products when a piece of equipment is found to be out of calibration.

Control of Nonconforming Product
(applies to 9001, 9002, and 9003)
The business should have a method of clearly identifying any product that does not conform to requirements. There must be a method for properly segregating nonconforming product from conforming product until a decision is made for its disposition or disposal. The procedure should define the authority of those responsible for making disposition. Records of all nonconformities and disposition of the nonconforming product must be maintained.

Corrective Action (applies to 9001 and 9002)
The business should have a method for analysis of nonconformances to determine trends and a procedure for investigation to assign

causes. A method is required to implement preventive measures and to ensure that all agreed-upon actions have been taken. Basically the system should enable investigation of the root cause of each problem and the method leading to the implementation of corrective action to prevent further problems.

Handling, Storage, Packaging, and Delivery (applies to 9001, 9002, and 9003)

A documented system is needed to assure the safety and maintenance of product quality during packaging, storage, and delivery. Special storage requirements must be defined, such as temperature or moisture protection or other customer or legal requirements. The documentation should ensure that the correct packaging material and method are used and that customer and legislative delivery conditions or requirements are met.

Quality Records (applies to 9001, 9002, and 9003)

The business should have a documented system for maintaining quality records for a set period of time. The system must consider customer and legal requirements.

Internal Quality Audits (applies to 9001 and 9002)

The business should have a documented method for performing quality audits on a scheduled, periodic basis. The audits should determine whether procedures are in place, whether they are adequate, whether they are being followed, and whether everyone involved is adequately trained to understand the requirements. The quality audit system should audit the corrective action procedures and provide for reports to management.

Training (applies to 9001, 9002, and 9003)

The business should have a documented program for training. The system should include a method for determining training needs, implementing training, and maintaining a history of the results of training. Training should cover product specifications, process methods, legal requirements, and inspection techniques.

Statistical Techniques (applies to 9001, 9002, and 9003)
The business should have documented procedures that take into account statistical techniques used to measure and evaluate product quality. Process capability and sampling must be considered.

Servicing (applies to 9001)
If applicable, the business should have a documented method for performing and verifying that product servicing meets specified requirements.

Implementation Plan
The following shows actions and their timing for a business that wishes to become certified to the ISO 9000 series of standards.

Action	Timing
	(months in advance of (–) or after (+) certification)
Top management assigns ISO task leader.	–18
Task leader selects team participants.	–18
Task team reviews the business, determines needs, and makes recommendations.	–17

Note: The task team should consider the business's customer requirements, the general trends for the business, and advantages and disadvantages of ISO certification. If the team concludes that ISO certification should be obtained, a budget and implementation plan should be developed.

Task team submits recommendation to top management.	–16

Top management decides if business
     is to be certified to ISO 9000.   −16

If top management decides to be
     certified, a certification team leader
     is announced.   −16

ISO team leader selects certification team.   −16

Certification team reviews business
     and identifies changes required.
     Assignments are set, and action
     is started.   −15

ISO leader and team select agency to
     perform certification.   −13

Note: Whoever is selected to perform the certification should be able to demonstrate that they have the authority to certify to ISO 9000.

ISO leader and team submit
     application for certification.   −13

Task team reviews progress monthly.
     Monthly reports of progress
     submitted to top management.   −13 to −6

Task team performs certification audit
     on the business or requests audit
     by independent group.   −6

Team reviews results and determines
     any additional work needed.
     Assignments are set, and action
     is reviewed once every two weeks.   −6 to −2

Team performs spot audits.	−1
Certifying agency performs audit and gives results.	0
Team reviews results and develops action plan and makes assignments for correction.	0
Certifying agency reaudits to verify correction, or response is sent to certifying agency.	+1
ISO task team verifies compliance with system.	continuous
Certifying agency reaudits.	every 6 months

Legal Aspects
Chapter 5

Resolving supplier issues in court is undesirable for both parties. It is expensive, time-consuming, has potential impact on either party's reputation, and is unpredictable. The only ones who are always well rewarded in court cases are the attorneys, who make their money regardless of the outcome.

The law and cases on contracts and purchasing are extensive. This chapter will discuss only those aspects of the law that relate to quality of purchased material. Although most purchasing agents and buyers are familiar with these legal issues, quality control people and design engineers are less likely to have acquired this knowledge. Since these people become involved in subcontracts, they should have some understanding of the laws. This background may be useful in preparing requirements, in dealings with suppliers, and in matters involving inspection, acceptance, and compliance of purchased commodities, services, or data.

Buyers and sellers are covered in their dealings by the Uniform Commercial Code (UCC). This code was prepared to provide consistency in buyer-seller relations and to remove some of the legal uncertainties regarding contractual disagreement. The following interpretations are based on a review of the code and numerous cases reported in recent journals.

Authority and Agency

The purchasing agent and buyer are legally considered agents for their company in that they are delegated the authority to act for the firm. They deal with salespersons who are considered agents of the supplier. As an agent of the company, a buyer is delegated the authority to act for the company in dealings with suppliers. Other persons, such as design engineers or quality control people, deal with their supplier counterparts but are not usually authorized to make binding agreements. The activities of the purchasing agent or buyer—who serves as the official representative or agent for the company in dealings with suppliers—fall under the *law of agency*. In simple words, an *agent* is someone who has been given the power to act for another person or organization, called the *principal*. An agency agreement should always specify the degree of authority that is delegated to the agent. This authority, however, can either be expressed and clearly stated or implied from the way the people act.

The purchasing agent, then, has the authority to bind the company (principal) to contracts. Most companies, however, make it clear to buyers just what they are authorized to do and exactly when higher approval is necessary.

Each person dealing with supplier personnel must recognize the scope of his or her own individual authority and make it known to the supplier's people involved. In this way, legally enforceable agreements will be created only by those so authorized. An unauthorized person who implies that he or she has the authority to make agreements may bind the company by actions or statements.

Contracts

A contract between the purchaser and the supplier contains the requirements for the goods and/or services to be supplied. The contract can be in the form of a purchase order or a more detailed document, depending on the degree of definition needed. Generally, more complex items require more description in the contract.

Elements of a Contract

Certain basic elements must be presented before a valid contract exists. There must be two or more parties to the contract. Also required is an offer by one party and acceptance by the other. The offer must identify—as a minimum—the price, quantity, subject matter, and parties. The acceptance must conform to all terms of the offer; any additional terms are considered a rejection of the original offer and the communication of a new offer. For example, a supplier offers to supply one hundred units that meet a given specification for $50,000, and the purchaser accepts the offer. The supplier would then be obligated to supply the items in accordance with the specification, and the purchaser would be obligated to pay the agreed amount. As another example, the promise by S to furnish a test is not a contract until accepted by B. Furthermore, to be a contract, it must state the consideration to be given by B, in the form of money, an act, or agreement to forbear action (such as agreement by B not to return a prior shipment of nonconforming items received from S).

In the typical contract, each party acknowledges agreement to the terms. Written agreements are preferred, but oral contracts are valid within legal definitions. A contract can be created by an offer by one party and an act by the other. For example, buyer Y offers to buy ten items, catalog No. 601, from supplier X. Supplier X receives the offer and ships the items. The act by X created an implied acceptance—a contract then came into existence.

Take another example where quality control and purchasing are both clearly involved. A purchase order agreement specifies fifty items at $100 each. Upon receipt, purchaser's receiving inspection discovers a nonconformance. The supplier then offers to reduce the price to $75 each if purchaser will keep half the shipment. The return of half the shipment to supplier would be an act of implied acceptance of the offer.

Assume a supplier publishes a catalog listing an item at $50 each. Buyer B responds with an order for ten items. Does a contract exist? Probably not. A catalog is usually considered a declaration of intent to receive offers. The supplier must accept each specific order before a contract exists.

Oral Contracts

If an oral contract can be proved, it is valid. Frequently, however, it is not easy to prove. Witnesses are one means of proving an oral agreement. Even if an oral contract can be proved, however, it will not stand up if (1) there is a written agreement with conflicting terms or (2) it falls into a category of contracts that the laws of the particular state specify must be in writing. Most state laws and the Uniform Commercial Code state that contracts involving $500 or more must be in writing to be enforceable. It is the best policy, of course, for a buyer and seller to make all agreements in writing to lessen the likelihood of later disagreements. There are certain legal requirements for creation of valid written contracts—such as an offer, an acceptance, and signatures of the parties. There is, however, some variability in the exact procedures.

Assume that a buyer and supplier's representative reach a verbal agreement. The UCC provides that when a seller sends a written confirmation stating the understanding of the verbal agreement, the buyer has ten days to give written notice of any objections. If no objections are given, both parties are bound to a contract. If the buyer responds with objections within the ten-day period, neither party is bound. In the later case, either party could then make a new offer and attempt to obtain agreement.

Differing Terms

If a purchaser supplies a specification or a written offer to purchase, these can be accepted or rejected by the supplier. Assume the supplier submits alternative terms, or sends an acknowledgment of the order containing differing terms. Based on legal custom and precedent, this is considered a counteroffer, and the original offer is terminated. It is then the buyer's turn to accept or reject the counteroffer. This acceptance can be express, or it may be implied by acceptance of the goods from the supplier.

The provision in the Uniform Commercial Code differs from this common-law concept. In the initial dealings, possibly following verbal discussion or agreement, the buyer may follow up with a purchase order to the supplier. Assume again that the purchase order specifies requirements and conditions. Then the supplier sends an acknowledgment accepting the offer but does so on the supplier's own form, which contains different terms. The UCC provides that the terms expressed on the acknowledgment become additional terms of the subcontract, unless (1) the original purchase order specifically objected in advance to any further terms, (2) the new terms make a substantial difference in the goods with respect to their usability, or (3) the buyer objects to the terms within a reasonable time.

A court upheld a subcontract clause on the acknowledgment which stated that no warranties were provided, even though the original purchase order specified that a warranty was to be provided as part of the order. The UCC usually operates to the advantage of the buyer in cases of differing terms, and the buyer can further protect the company by taking the following precautions with respect to the purchase order:

1. The order should expressly limit acceptance to "the terms herein. Any additional or different terms proposed by the seller are hereby rejected."
2. In each original purchase order, object to all "other terms" in advance. Use a clause such as "The only contractual terms with the supplier are those found in this purchase order."

3. Examine acknowledgments and other forms closely.
4. Include an arbitration clause.
5. Specify ownership of any documents created.
6. Include a dispute-resolution agreement.
7. If buyer and seller are in different states, specify which state law will control.

Furthermore, promptly object to any unacceptable clauses. If the supplier ships the goods without recognition of the objection, don't accept or use the goods until the objection is resolved.

Firm Offers

Upon receipt of an offer by a supplier to furnish goods at a specific price, the buyer may need to delay acceptance in order to check other vendors for price, and also check within the company for technical acceptability of the goods offered. The UCC provides that when a supplier makes a written offer in response to a request for bid (or request for quotation), and also sets a time during which it will hold the offer open, the supplier cannot retract the offer before the specified date. If no time limit is specified, the offer remains open for a reasonable time (but not over three months). This provision of the UCC gives the buyer assurance that he or she can evaluate the bids received and award the contract without the risk that the offer may be withdrawn in the meantime.

Honest Mistakes

Mistakes can occur in the preparation of a purchase agreement, specification or bid. Of course, considerable care should be exercised to avoid errors, since they are not always easily corrected. If there were an error and the dispute could not be settled without litigation, however, the conditions of the particular case would determine its outcome. Generally, a mistake by only one party to the contract does not make the contract void unless the other party is aware of the mistake or should have been aware of it. As an illustration, consider the following examples:

A supplier intends to quote a price of $950, but through a typing error instead quotes $910, which is transmitted to the purchaser. If the buyer accepts the offer without knowledge of the error, a court will probably hold that a valid contract exists.

If, in the above case, the price was typed in error as $95, a court would probably hold that the buyer should have recognized the error and that, therefore, the contract is void.

Minor mutual mistakes in the contract do not affect its validity. Factual errors that materially affect the agreement, however, would render the agreement void. For example, buyer B agrees in the contract to purchase the remaining five units of Model X test equipment at a reduced price. Unknown to the buyer and seller, the units were severely damaged by fire yesterday. The contract would be void.

A buyer or seller should not assume that an error will result in a void contract. Therefore, extremely care must be taken in preparation of the document.

Reasonable Time

Schedules or dates for a supplier's action are usually specified in the purchase order. Courts seldom set aside time requirements as being unreasonable if both parties have agreed to them. Where a time is not specified in the contract, the UCC and courts will decide whether the action took place in a "reasonable time."

The time allowed for acceptance or rejection of material by a purchaser is often a subject of controversy. Another area of controversy can be the time allowed for acceptance of an offer made by a supplier. A buyer who waited seven months, for example, and then accepted a supplier's offer was said by a court to have waited too long. It was not considered a reasonable length of time.

In another case, five months was found to be considered a reasonable period of time to reject defective goods. In this case, the buyer had identified a problem with the goods when received. The supplier had given assurance that the problem would be taken care of and sent a representative to observe the defects but never corrected them. Under these circumstances, then, the court held that five months was not an unreasonable period of time for rejection.

Precedents can be established by actions taken in prior situations. If in the past, for example, a supplier had taken back goods after the purchaser had them for forty-five days, this could establish forty-five days as a reasonable time even if the contract specified thirty days for acceptance. Usual and customary practices in the particular trade also work to establish reasonable times. In each case, however, a court will observe any factors that may cause the case at hand to be unique.

Shipment and Receipt

Authorization to Ship

Often a contract specifies a method of packing and shipment. If there is no provision in the contract, the purchaser, according to the Uniform Commercial Code, may designate the method. The law, however, expects the buyer and the seller to cooperate toward meeting the overall objective of the purchase order. What if the seller notified the buyer that goods were ready for shipment and requested instructions and/or authorization? The purchaser is required to provide these instructions. Failure to do so can be considered a breach of the contract by the purchaser. In general, a court will expect both parties to cooperate.

In cases where the supplier has goods ready for shipment, but the buyer has the responsibility to furnish instructions and does not do so within a reasonable time, the seller can do any of the following:

1. Proceed to ship by a reasonable method
2. Sell the goods to a third party and claim damages from the buyer if the price obtained is less than the contract price
3. Claim breach of agreement and cancel the purchase order
4. Expect to obtain a valid reason for delay in shipment

In its decision, a court will consider whether each party is attempting to cooperate to achieve the requirements of the purchase order.

Goods in Separate Lots

Many contracts involve the shipment of goods in separate shipments, or lots. The UCC defines an installment contract as one that specifies or permits delivery of the goods in separate lots to be accepted or rejected separately. Receiving inspectors, quality control personnel, the design engineer, the production schedulers, and buying agent can become involved in acceptance/rejection decisions involving individual lots. Therefore, legal implications are often significant to each of these persons.

A contract can specify schedules for deliveries in lots. However, deliveries in installments can also arise by specific agreement between parties or based on certain circumstances—such as when the supplier has insufficient items available. Any installment may be rejected by the purchaser for nonconformities. The buyer also has other options as discussed later that apply to acceptance or rejection of any shipment. Sometimes a purchaser will allege that nonconformance of a lot or installment affects the value of the entire contract and that, therefore, a contract breach has occurred. The provisions of the UCC are based on the concept that the contract should be preserved as long as an undue burden is not placed on either party. Beyond that, if the buyer and seller cannot reach an agreement, the case will have to be settled in court.

The court considers all aspects of a case. In one instance, a contract provided for deliveries of two hundred units per month for twelve months. Some shipments were as much as three weeks late, and two shipments were rejected for nonconformities. The purchaser wrote, canceling the contract, and the supplier filed a countersuit for damages, citing changes in design requirements as a cause of the delays. In finding for the supplier, the court pointed out that (1) there was no evidence of the buyer showing concern over earlier delayed shipments, (2) the supplier had replaced all rejected items, and (3) there were changes in requirements subsequent to the original schedule. In any case, courts look unfavorably on purchasers who do not cooperate toward resolving problems related to defects. The supplier, however, remains responsible for costs related to defective or nonconforming products.

A buyer can lose the right, by law, to claim a breach in the overall contract for a particular nonconformity if he or she accepts any lots with that nonconformity without notifying the supplier of an intent to claim contract breach.

Special Tooling

In many contracts, the purchase order requires that special production or inspection tooling be made for the order. The terms of the purchase order will govern the ownership of the tooling and the date payment is due. Unless specified otherwise, the supplier can expect payment and bill the buyer when the tooling is completed and proven (or inspected). It is not necessary that the tooling be received at the purchaser's facility.

Delays in Performance

Delays can occur in delivery, service, inspection, testing, or other task identified by date in the purchase order. If any requirements are not met by the specified date, the UCC considers it a breach of contract, except where compliance in good faith with a government order or directive—domestic or foreign—caused the delay, or an event occurs beyond the control of the supplier that the buyer and seller assumed would not occur. In either case, if the supplier has some items, but not enough to meet outstanding orders, the available items must be allocated among all contracts.

When a buyer receives notification from a supplier that delivery will be delayed indefinitely, the buyer is allowed to terminate any unfulfilled portions of the agreement. The term *cover* is defined as a buyer's discretionary right to buy goods elsewhere when the seller wrongfully fails to deliver the goods as required under the contract (UCC Section 2-712). What if a buyer is insecure and anticipates a breach in contract? The buyer has the right to demand written assurance from the seller that the contract will be fulfilled.

Title to Goods

When the purchasing company takes title to goods, the purchaser assumes responsibility for risks or damages that may subsequently occur to the goods. If the goods are shipped F.O.B. the seller's facility, the purchaser takes title when the carrier takes the goods. The seller is, however, obligated to follow the buyer's instructions in the contract as to packaging and shipping, or to utilize reasonable packaging and packing methods.

Risk of Loss

The UCC provides that when not otherwise agreed, the risk of loss passes to the buyer on receipt of the goods. This places the responsibility for shipping damage, theft, or destruction upon the seller or the transporting agent up until the time the buyer receives them.

What if the customer requested the seller to hold the goods past the date of intended shipment? In a recent case, the supplier allowed the customer to leave purchased goods on the supplier's property for a few days. During those few days the goods were severely damaged, and the purchaser refused to take them, claiming that the vendor was responsible. The court held that since the parties did not have any agreement on the risk of loss, and the vendor could have required the buyer to accept the risk before allowing the delay in pickup of the goods, the vendor was responsible for loss according to provisions in the UCC.

Inspection and Acceptance of Goods

The terms of the contract concerning inspection and acceptance govern the place, time and/or method of inspection. In any case, the buyer is entitled to inspect all goods to determine conformance to requirements. *Nonconforming goods* are those not in accordance with any obligation under a contract (UCC section 2-106[2]). The law gives the buyer the right to perform this inspection before payment is made, unless there is an agreement to the contrary.

The costs of performing the inspection are the responsibility of the purchaser, unless the contract specifies otherwise or the inspection reveals that items do not conform to the requirements. Also, the buyer is entitled to recover costs related to return of the nonconforming items plus damages suffered—such as those resulting from a customer's cancellation of the order.

Acceptance or Rejection

If the goods do not conform to any requirements, the purchaser has the following options:

1. Reject the entire lot or shipment
2. Accept a portion of the shipment and reject part (However, normal commercial unites, such as drums of oil, cannot be divided without the seller's permission.)
3. Accept the shipment as is, or accept it subject to a reduction in price

The purchaser has certain obligations when rejecting material. Failure to fulfill these obligations may result in the purchaser's loss of the right to return the material.

1. The seller must be notified of the rejection promptly or within a reasonable time of the discovery of the nonconformity. The term *cure* refers to the right of the seller to remedy nonconforming goods shipped to the buyer prior to the date final performance of the contract is to take place (UCC section 2-508).
2. The buyer must specify what the nonconformity is and how it was determined.
3. The buyer must request instructions from the supplier for disposition of the goods and hold them for a reasonable time.
4. The buyer must carry out any instructions given by the supplier regarding disposition of the nonconforming material.

A purchaser has a reasonable period during which to accept or reject shipments, or the materials may be presumed to be accepted. If a shipment is accepted, the buyer becomes obligated to pay, and the ability to later reject is waived if the reasons for rejection could have been observed during a reasonable inspection. Defects later discovered are valid reasons for revoking the acceptance if the defects could not have been easily determined upon receipt. In any case, the purchaser is obligated to notify the supplier promptly whenever the nonconformities are discovered. If, however, the buyer indicates rejection but goes ahead and uses the material in question, acceptance is deemed to have occurred. On the other hand, if the seller induced the purchaser to accept a shipment without inspection by assurances that the material conformed, the purchaser may retain rights to reject later.

In some instances, a supplier will send parts or materials on approval or some other basis, stating that the receiver has a reasonable time to try them and/or decide whether to keep them. In this case, the receiver has a reasonable amount of time to decide upon acceptance or return. The buyer has this option whether or not the goods conform.

Buyers' Rights—Example

A unit arrived from the supplier but failed to meet the specifications in the contract. Notified of the problem, the supplier attempted but failed to correct it. The purchaser had placed a deposit on the unit, but agreed that if the deposit were returned, no other action against the supplier would be taken. The supplier, however, refused to return the deposit. The purchaser found another unit that he purchased from a different supplier at a higher price and filed suit against the seller to recover the deposit plus the price differential.

The court awarded the buyer the deposit return plus the price difference, saying that the buyer's offer to settle for return of the deposit was based on immediate return of the deposit. Furthermore, a purchaser has the right to seek replacements when goods do not conform to the contract requirements.

Revoking Acceptance

The buyer has the right to revoke a prior acceptance if (1) the buyer's acceptance of nonconforming goods was based on a reasonable inspection that did not reveal the defects or (2) the buyer accepted nonconforming goods under the reasonable assumption that the nonconformity would be corrected, and it was not corrected within a reasonable time. A revocation of an acceptance must occur within a reasonable time after discovery of the nonconformity, and it cannot occur after the goods have been substantially changed in condition from causes other than the original defect.

Inspection Clauses—Complex Equipment

Standard inspection clauses usually appear in purchase orders for complex equipment. The following clauses are typical:

> 1. All supplies shall be subject to inspection and test by the purchaser to the extent practicable at all times and places including the period of manufacture, and in any event prior to acceptance.
> 2. In case any supplies or lots of supplies are defective in material or workmanship or otherwise not in conformity with the requirements of this contract, the purchaser shall have the right either to reject them (with or without instructions as to their disposition) or to require their correction. Supplies or lots of supplies that have been rejected or required to be corrected shall be removed or, if permitted or required by the purchaser, corrected in place by and at the expense of the supplier promptly after notice, and shall not thereafter be tendered for acceptance unless the former rejection or requirement of correction is disclosed. If the supplier fails to promptly remove such supplies or to replace or correct such supplies, the purchaser either (i) may replace or correct such supplies and charge to the supplier the cost occasioned; or (ii) may terminate the contract for default as

provided in the clause of this contract entitled "Default." Unless the supplier corrects or replaces such supplies within the time specified in the delivery schedule, the purchaser may take the delivery of such supplies at a reduction in price that is equitable under the circumstances.

3. If any inspection or test is made by the purchaser on the premises of the supplier, the supplier without additional charge shall provide all reasonable facilities and assistance for the safety and convenience of the purchaser's inspectors in the performance of their duties. All inspections and tests by the purchaser shall be performed in such a manner as not to unduly delay the work. The purchaser reserves the right to charge to the supplier any additional cost of purchaser's inspection and test when supplies are not ready at the time such inspection and test is requested or when reinspection or retest is necessitated by prior rejection.

4. Acceptance or rejection of the supplies shall be made as promptly as practicable after delivery, except as otherwise provided in this contract; but failure to inspect and accept or reject supplies shall neither relive the supplier from responsibility for such supplies that are not in accordance with the contract requirements nor impose liability on the purchaser therefor. The inspection and test by the purchaser of any supplies or lots thereof do not relieve the supplier from any responsibility regarding defects or other failures to meet the contract requirements that may be discovered prior to acceptance. Except as otherwise provided in this contract, acceptance shall be conclusive except as regards latent defects, fraud, or such gross mistakes as amount to fraud.

5. The supplier shall provide and maintain an inspection system acceptable to the purchaser covering the supplies hereunder. Records of all inspection work by the supplier shall be kept complete and available to the purchaser during the performance of

this contract and for such longer period as may be specified elsewhere in this contract.

Arbitration

Where problems involving contract disputes between buyer and supplier cannot be resolved, either party can bring suit. Some contracts
call for arbitration by a third party to settle the dispute, or both parties
may agree to arbitration rather than have the disagreement go to litigation. When there is such an agreement, the arbitration becomes
binding.

Fraud

It is important to briefly review the definition of fraud as it may
impact on quality. Any misrepresentation of the quality or performance of supplied goods can be considered fraud if all of the following are true?

1. The misrepresentation was made before the contract agree-
    ment was signed.
2. The statement in question was untrue, and the seller knew it
    to be untrue or made it recklessly.
3. The misrepresentation was made for the purpose of induc-
    ing the other party to act on it.
4. The other party did, in fact, rely on the misrepresentation.
5. The other party was damaged by the reliance.

Thus we can see that (1) a false statement made after the contract
was signed is not fraud, (2) if the seller was expressing an opinion on
quality, it would not constitute fraud, and (3) if the buyer or the
buyer's representative has previously inspected the goods that are the
subject of a misrepresentation, the purchaser may have assumed
responsibility. The latter is true, however, only if the purchaser has
the skill and ability to ascertain that a particular defect existed.
Generally, the purchaser has a right to reject materials at a later date
for previously undiscovered defects.

Warranties

Quality exists if material conforms to the requirements at the time of acceptance. Reliability exists if this conformance continues for a specified period of time. A *warranty* is a guarantee by the seller to the purchaser that the goods are or shall be as represented. The UCC defines warranty as any affirmation of fact, express or implied, by a seller of goods to the buyer as part of a contract of sale (UCC sections 2-312 to 2-315). A warranty usually specifies that a product will continue to meet some or all the requirements for a specified period of time. It also defines the actions to be taken if the product fails to perform as promised.

Express or Implied Warranties

Warranties can be either express or implied. Warranties specifically given by the manufacturer can be stated in contracts, purchase orders, advertisements, or catalogs. They can be written or oral, but written warranties are preferred since there is less room for disagreement on the intention. Although it is better to have warranty agreements formally stated in the contract, statements in letters or other communication are sufficient. In a recent case, a supplier's oral warranty was recorded on tape. The court said it was valid even though it exceeded the standard written warranty made by the supplier. Usually, however, for an oral warranty to be valid, a company must have done one of the following: (1) notified the buyer of the salesperson's authorization to make the guarantee, (2) confirmed the guarantee, or (3) maintained a tradition of accepting responsibility for salespersons' guarantees in past dealings. Courts have recognized that salespersons tend to "puff" their products, so care is required in separating "puffing" from a guarantee.

Whether a written warranty exists or not, there is always an *implied warranty* by a supplier that the goods or services are fit for the ordinary purposes for which they are intended. In addition, if the buyer informs the seller of the specific use for which the goods are intended, and relies on the seller's knowledge and judgment, there is an implied warranty that the goods will be reasonably fit for that specific purpose. If an express warranty conflicts with the implied terms, the express warranty governs. Implied warranties are covered as part of the UCC (sections 2-312 to 2-315) as shown in Figure 5.1.

To take maximum advantage of the implied warranty of fitness for use, a buyer should make technical information on use available to the supplier, seek the supplier's advice on specifications, and have the supplier's representatives meet with users for discussion of usage.

Time Is a Factor

Although a warranty may extend for a period of time, the purchaser has the obligation to make a claim to the supplier as soon as product or service deficiencies are recognized. Courts have thrown out cases in which the purchaser took an unreasonable amount of time to determine that a condition of deficiency existed. If a deficiency could be easily observed at receiving inspection, a later claim may be invalid. This is especially true if the supplier specifies a limit on the time—such as 30 days—during which a claim can be made.

Many deficiencies, however, cannot be ascertained until the items have been assembled into larger units, or are later tested or placed in actual use. Many warranties state that the goods will continue to work as intended for a specified period of time after being placed in use.

Denial of Implied Warranty

A supplier may deny that an implied warranty of merchantability or fitness for use exists, but the supplier must do this in a conspicuous manner. Disclaimers in small print on the back of documents or on the printed form are not considered sufficient. If the seller intends to disclaim a warranty of merchantability or fitness for use, the contract must use those words or other language, clearly stating that there are no implied warranties. A disclaimer must be in print larger than the rest of the document, in a different color, or in contrasting type to catch the buyer's eye.

In a recent decision, a Pennsylvania Supreme Court ruling indicated that a supplier must be very specific in contract language if it desires to disclaim a warranty. The court ruled that an implied warranty

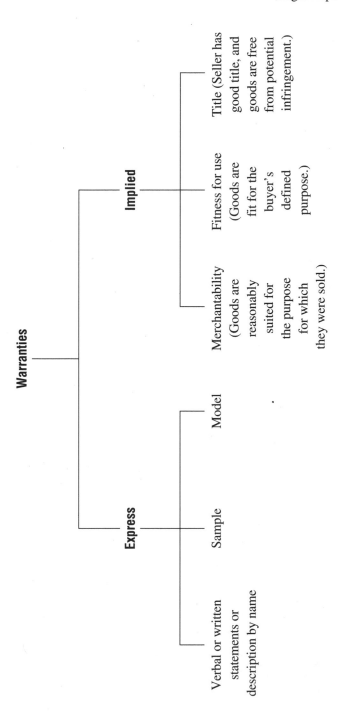

Figure 5.1   Categories of warranties as defined in the UCC.

of *merchantability* under UCC section 2-316 cannot be excluded unless the term *merchantability* is used. Also, an implied warranty of fitness for a particular use can only be excluded if the contract states that no warranties exist beyond the face of the agreement. Terms such as *as is* or *with all faults* represent typical statements of disclaimer, but they must be conspicuous to be valid.

UCC and Warranties
The UCC deals at length with warranties and promises by the supplier and the purchaser. In general, the UCC supports the buyer who places faith in statements provided by the supplier. The terms provide that an express warranty is created as follows:

1. Promises made by the supplier to the buyer are valid and shall be complied with.
2. Descriptions of the materials furnished are a warranty that the goods will conform to these descriptions.
3. Samples of the goods supplied during the bargaining process imply that the goods supplied are to conform to the sample.

The legal complexities of the UCC present some difficulties to the buyer, design engineer, and quality control engineer as follows:

1. Where an offer is made in writing, the seller must live up to it for the time specified.
2. Oral agreements are binding but are often difficult to prove, so it is best to confirm them in writing.
3. Terms stated in the specifications and purchase order which conflict with seller's disclaimers or terms in acknowledgments are usually resolved by courts in the buyer's favor.
4. A buyer can expect items furnished to be fit for the intended use.

The UCC also addresses cases in which a disclaimer is inconsistent with an express warranty in the contract. Here, the UCC states clearly that the warranty governs if there is any inconsistency.

These UCC provisions provide some peace of mind: the buyer can depend on express or implied warranties without having to worry about trick phrases or small print in unusual places.

Product Liability

The number of lawsuits brought against manufacturers for product liability began to increase rapidly in the 1950s, and in recent years has reached over 100,000 annually, often with large awards. Courts have tended to take the position that there is an implied representation that a product is safe, sometimes regardless of how it was used. Furthermore, courts have tended to use the principle of "strict liability," meaning that the manufacturer rather than the injured parties should bear the costs of injuries due to defective products. Published disclaimers with regard to product safety by manufacturers have been relatively ineffective in jury trials.

Apparently, a manufacturer's best defense is to eliminate possible causes of injuries from the product, even going to the extent of considering unusual or unexpected uses of the product. Evidence of a company policy and organized approach to product safety helps provide a defense in lawsuits. This organized approach would include addressing safety considerations in design review, instituting a sound quality control program, carefully considering product labels, and avoiding making unrealistic claims in advertising. A company should also collect safety data on products and get feedback through customer service of problems in actual product use. In contracting with a supplier, companies should take care that specifications and contracts contain adequate provisions passing on product safety requirements to suppliers. Consideration for safety should be part of the supplier evaluation and selection process.

Tools for Quality Improvement

Chapter 6

Several good books explain in detail how to use various statistical and other tools in quality improvement. In this chapter, the objective is to mention these tools and provide enough information to understand when to use and how to prepare or interpret each type of tool. Some of these tools require measurement data, whereas others do not. Any person involved in supplier surveys or audits should know enough about each tool to determine whether it is being used properly in a supplier's facility. Other chapters in this book will use some of these tools to illustrate points.

The following tools for quality improvement will be described in this chapter.

1. *Brainstorming*—This technique is used to define problems and generate potential solutions for the problem.
2. *Histogram*—This technique is used to create a visual picture of a process and show its center and variability (spread). It is also used to show relation to the process specification limits.

3. *Process-flow diagram*—This technique is used to display knowledge about a process, interaction among elements in the process, and identify possible control points in the process.
4. *Fishbone, or cause-and-effect, diagram*—This technique displays contributing factors and their interrelationship, separating process factors such as material, method, people, and procedure.
5. *Run chart*—This technique displays process measurements in relation to time. It helps in recognizing unexpected problems.
6. *Control chart*—This technique is used to monitor a process over time and identify trends or out-of-control conditions.
7. *Scatter diagram*—This technique displays the relationship between two variables.
8. *Pareto diagram*—This technique identifies the most significant (vital few) problems to be worked on first.
9. *Design of experiments*—This technique is used in product design and process development to identify magnitudes of interaction among process variables.

The following concepts are helpful in understanding the use of these tools for quality improvement:

- Problem analysis is based on the idea that a problem is caused by a change. If the change can be identified, the problem could be controlled or corrected. Note that correction of a condition also involves change. Since change is the cause of a problem, the change mechanism needs analysis to ensure that the improvement will not also be viewed as a problem.
- Process analysis is based on the idea that each process has a customer and a supplier. Both could be within a company (i.e., the internal customer who uses the output of a process.)

In addition, factors such as procedures, people, equipment, and method affect each of these factors and, therefore, the outcome of the process.

- Process analysis is further based on the idea that each measurable parameter varies. By analyzing the variation, we can understand the parameter and calculate whether the process has an unreasonable variation or whether the variation is "normal." If an unreasonable variation is detected, then some factor caused the unreasonable variation. Investigating and controlling the factor causing the unreasonable variation will improve the performance of the process.

- Improvement can occur by eliminating unnecessary variation.

Brainstorming

This tool helps identify as many ideas as possible in a short time concerning a problem or situation. Those most involved with the problem should participate.

Method:
1. Set up a group meeting.
2. Select an individual to write down the ideas.
3. Identify the topic or problem to be analyzed.
4. Either go from person to person in sequence or have an unstructured approach, and let participants give their ideas of what the problem is or the possible solution. Write down the ideas.
5. Regardless of the idea expressed, do not editorialize or criticize the idea. All ideas are good from a brainstorming standpoint. Sometimes the more obtuse ideas help others think freely or lead the way to the real problem.
6. The brainstorming session lasts for only a short time—typically five to fifteen minutes.

7. After the brainstorming session is completed, analyze the results to identify the apparent problem or problems to work on or the most likely solution.

Histogram

A histogram is used to display a distribution of data. The Pareto chart is a special type of histogram that will be presented later. If constructed properly, the histogram reveals the degree of process variation.

For many processes, the histogram should show the greatest number of data points near the center, with roughly an equal number on either side of the center. A histogram that does not look like that is considered to be skewed.

By studying the spread and center of the histogram in relation to requirements, the capability of the process to produce a product meeting the requirements can be determined.

Method:
1. Determine the type of data to be taken. The type of data used in a histogram is generally referred to as *variable data*. Conditions such as temperature and dimensions are examples of variable data.
2. Decide on the degree of accuracy to be used to measure the variable data. If the accuracy is not sufficient, no variation will be measurable. If the accuracy is too detailed, the cost generally will be high and the difficulty of collecting data increases.
3. Gather the data.
4. Count the number of data points in the data set. This number will be referred to as N.
5. Determine the range of the entire data set. To determine the range, take the largest data value and subtract from it the lowest data value. This number will be referred to as R.

6. Divide the data range into a certain number of cells or classes. It is best to keep the number of cells or classes no lower than six and no higher than fifteen. This number will be referred to as K. Several attempts may be needed to achieve the best distribution for analysis.

7. Determine the class width (H) by using the following calculation: $H = R/K$. Round off the value of H, but carry the value to one more decimal point than the data gathered. This will assure that no data value will fall into more than one cell or class.

8. Determine the class end points by taking the smallest individual measurement in the data set. For each subsequent class end point, add on the value of H calculated in Step 7.

9. Construct a frequency table based on the values computed in the prior steps. The horizontal axis represents the variable. The vertical axis represents the quantity of measurements falling into each cell.

10. Construct the histogram using the data as in Figure 6.1. Place the data in the appropriate cells. Each data point in a cell should increase the height of the cell by equal increments. Continue to construct the histogram until all the data points are entered.

11. Examine the results and determine if, based on experience, they are reasonable. For example, analyze the spread, average (center), and shape. Do the data suddenly stop, or does more than one peak occur? Based on the observations, additional studies can be formulated. For the histogram example, the data looks to be single moded and reasonably spread. Visually, nothing looks unusual so far.

A histogram such as would look unusual.

12. On the horizontal axis, draw the specification limits. Compare the histogram with the specification. Are the measurements centered within the limits? Is the spread such that

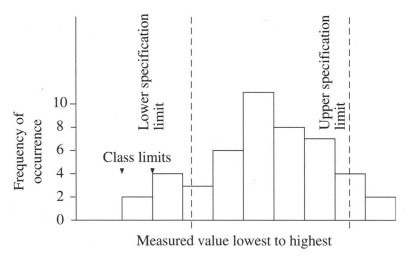

Figure 6.1   Histogram.

parts will meet the requirements of the engineering drawing? In Figure 6.1, the process variability is resulting in out-of-specification parts. Further calculations of process capability are shown in Appendix 6A to this chapter.

Process-Flow Diagram

The process-flow diagram is used to identify the actual and the ideal path a product or service follows. It also can be used to identify all the steps a product or service follows or must follow. Analysis of the diagram can uncover loopholes or redundancies. Flow diagrams provide an excellent method for studying planned processes or for procedure preparation. Figure 6.2 uses a flow diagram to illustrate the steps in preparing and analyzing a process-flow diagram.

Method:
1. Define the boundaries of the process clearly.
2. Decide on the symbols to be used. Note that simple, easily recognizable symbols are best.

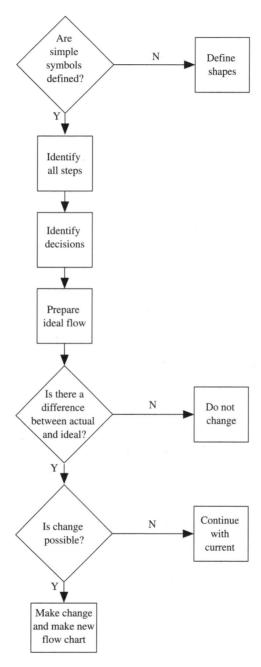

Figure 6.2   Process-flow diagram.

3. Use the symbols and document the flow of the process.
4. Be sure that each feedback loop has an escape.
5. Each process box usually has one output arrow. If not, a decision diamond might be required.

Fishbone Diagram

The fishbone, or cause-and-effect, diagram is used to show the rela-tionship between cause and effect (see Figure 6.3). It provides a method for analyzing the major factors affecting an output. The fishbone diagram usually consists of four main bones (ribs) attached to the backbone. These main bones analyze personnel, machine, method, and material. The effects of environment on each of these are also taken into consideration or added as a separate backbone. Other backbones can be considered if applicable.

Method:
1. Label the problem, or effect, on the right-hand side of the diagram.
2. Draw the causal factor, or backbone, from left to right.
3. Brainstorm for major causes leading to the effect.
4. Draw in the major causes, or main bones (ribs), and label appropriately.
5. Now brainstorm for causes of the main bones. This process will identify intermediate causes, or middle bones.
6. Add these middle bones to the diagram.
7. Examine the diagram carefully and once again brainstorm to identify minor causes, additions, or changes to the existing diagram bones.
8. Add minor causes, or small bones, to the chart.
9. Brainstorm ways to change the system and eliminate the causes permanently. Unless the system is changed, the improvement will not last.

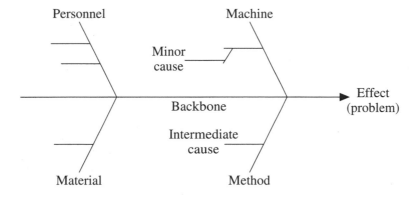

Figure 6.3   Fishbone, or cause-and-effect, diagram.

Run Chart

Run charts are used to display trends over time in a simple fashion. They provide a visual representation of the data and are used to monitor a process to determine if the process average is changing over time. Because it offers a view of a trend over time, the sequence of the data is critical. Run charts are commonly used to show yield, scrap, or machine downtime. Caution: Simple run charts can reveal every variation in data—even minor—and have the danger of causing reaction to every variation.

Method:
1. Construct a graph as in Figure 6.4. The horizontal side of the graph is the X axis; the vertical side is the Y axis.
2. Use the X axis to represent time. Time increases from left to right. Mark off the axis in an appropriate scale—for instance, hours or half days.
3. Use the Y axis to represent your variable. Value increases from bottom to top. Mark off the axis in an appropriate

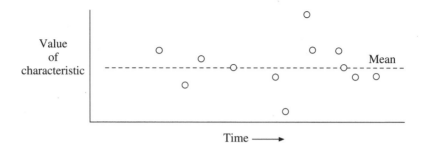

Figure 6.4   Run chart.

scale. Draw a central line showing the process mean from past experience or from the specification.

4. Make a measurement and note the time. Mark the point on the graph in an appropriate location.

5. Continue to make measurements and mark points on the graph in the appropriate locations (as in Figure 6.4). Remember that the sequence is important.

6. Observe the results. A trend of six or more points steadily increasing or decreasing with no reversals indicates significant change and the need for investigation. Nine consecutive points on one side of the mean indicate an abnormal event, a change in the average, and the need for an investigation. Based on the analysis, if the shift is unfavorable, take corrective action to eliminate it. If it is favorable, make the shift a permanent part of the process. For the data shown in Figure 6.4 a normal condition exists.

Control Chart

Control charts provide statistical control over a process by uncovering significant process variations. These charts are less sensitive than the run chart in showing every change in the process. The chart contains a centerline and upper and lower control limits on Figure 6.5. The control limits help separate specific causes from random causes of variation normally present in a process.

Caution must be taken using a control chart, because a process can be in statistical control and still produce product that is out of engineering specifications. Sometimes the control chart can also exhibit an "out of control" indication even though the change is an improvement. Such a condition could indicate either a need for corrective action or an opportunity to make a permanent improvement in the process.

Control charts fall into two categories:

1. Variables control charts measure an actual, continuous variable in such units as centimeters, ounces, degrees centigrade, or other continuous measurable quantities.
2. Other charts plot discrete values (whole numbers such as 1, 2, 3, 4) or values derived from counting rather than measuring.

Table 6.1 shows some of the most widely used types of control charts.

The details for preparing these charts are given in standard statistical quality control books. However, brief instructions for $\overline{X}$-R charts are given in Appendix 6B to this chapter.

Scatter Diagram

A scatter diagram is used to display visually the relationship of one variable to another. It can be used to test for possible cause-and-effect relationships by varying one variable (X) and measuring the results on the second variable (Y). The plot gives a visual clue to the

Table 6.1   Types of control charts.

Chart Type	Quantity Recorded	Application
Variables charts		
$\overline{X}$-R	Mean and range	Distance, weight, strength, time, and other similar variables
X chart	Individual values	Also called a run chart
Count (or attributes) charts		
p chart	Fraction defective	Charts defectives in varying size samples (fraction defective)
c chart	Number of defects	Charts the number of defects in a unit such as a plate of glass, an automobile, or a page of written material
np chart	Number of defective units	Charts defects in fixed size samples
u chart	Number of defects/area	Charts the number of defects on a product of varying size such as rolls of wire or bolts of fabric

1. Victor E. Kane, *Defect Prevention* (Milwaukee, Wis.: Quality Press, 1989).
2. Kazuo Ozeki and Tetsuichi Asaka, *Handbook of Quality Tools* (Cambridge, Mass.: Productivity Press, 1990).

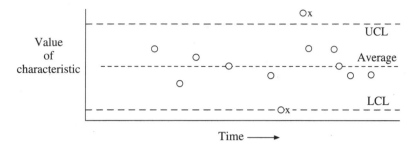

Time ⟶

UCL = Upper Control Limit
LCL = Lower Control Limit

Note:
The data points marked "x" are statistically improbable and
represent a process out of control. Evaluation of the process
should occur to determine why. For example, was a setting
changed, new material introduced, etc.?

Figure 6.5   Control chart.

strength of the relationship. The scatter diagram cannot, however,
prove that one variable causes the other.

As an example we may wish to check the relationship between
plating thickness and plating current.

Method:
1. Use a graph format with the X axis representing one vari-
    able and the Y axis representing the second variable.
2. Plot the values of the results of each measurement (see
    Figure 6.6).
3. Evaluate the result of the plotted points. Determine if there is
    a straight-line relation or another relation represented. A
    straight line, such as in Figure 6.6, shows that as X increases,
    Y increases also.

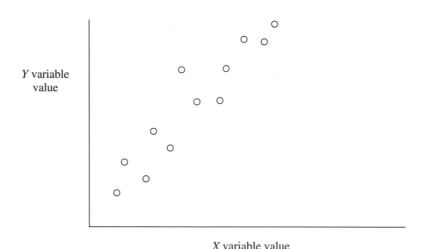

X variable value

Figure 6.6   Scatter diagram.

Pareto Diagram

The Pareto diagram is a simple method used to distinguish the vital problems from the large mass of problems. It is a specialized histogram. The term *Pareto diagram* (as in Figure 6.7) comes from the name of an Italian financier who recognized that 80 percent of the costs come from 20 percent of the sources. Dr. J. M. Juran expanded this idea to problem analysis.

Method:
1. Select the problems to be compared and ranked by brainstorming and/or using existing data.
2. Select the standard for comparison or unit of measurement—for example, annual cost or frequency.
3. Select a time period to be studied—for example, ten days, eight hours, four weeks.

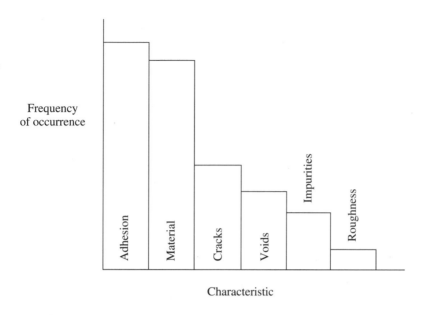

Figure 6.7   Pareto chart.

4. Gather necessary data—for example, defect A occurred X times in the last six months.

5. Compare the frequency of each category relative to all other categories—for example, defects due to adhesion happened 104 times as compared to 27 for impurities.

6. List the categories from left to right on the horizontal axis in order of decreasing frequency or cost. The categories containing the fewest items can be combined into an "other" category, which is placed on the extreme right as the last bar.

7. Above each classification or category, draw a rectangle whose height represents the frequency or cost in that classification.

8. Identify methods for reducing the highest item.
9. Once the highest item is reduced, a new Pareto analysis is done to identify the next highest. Note that a new analysis may be needed, since other conditions may have been introduced in the process of eliminating the first condition.

Design of Experiments

Design of experiments (DOE) is a statistical technique used to identify the magnitudes of interactions among important elements and among process variables. DOE is useful in product design and development, process development, and troubleshooting. DOE provides an efficient method to determine effects of variables by reducing the number of runs needed to arrive at decisions. The methods are very involved. Further explanation is beyond the scope of this book.

Using the Histogram for Determining Process Capability

Appendix 6A

Process Capability Index (C_p)

General: The process capability index (C_p) measures the capability of the process to meet specifications. To determine this, the following parameters are needed:

$$USL = \text{Upper specification limit}$$
$$LSL = \text{Lower specification limit}$$
$$MTD = \text{Mid-tolerance dimension} = (USL + LSL)/2$$
$$T = \text{Tolerance} = |USL - LSL|$$

In addition, the process capability for the actual process is needed. This can be calculated by the following formula:

$$\sigma = \sqrt{\frac{\Sigma\,(x - \bar{x})^2}{n - 1}} \quad \text{or} \quad \left(6\sigma = 6\sqrt{\frac{\Sigma\,(x - \bar{x})^2}{n - 1}} \right)$$

The C_p is then computed by the following:

$$C_p = T/6\,\sigma$$

This value is the first benchmark to determining whether a process is capable of meeting the specifications. This index provides a relationship of the allowable process spread compared to the actual process variation. Generally speaking, a value of $C_p = 1.33$ or higher means the process is capable of meeting the specification limits.

The C_p factor does not determine if the process is centered. The factor C_{pk} (process performance index) is used to determine if the process is centered in the specification limits. Since the tolerance is generally two-sided, a C_{pk} factor is calculated for both sides as follows:

$$C_{pk} = (USL - \bar{X})/3\,\sigma \qquad \text{or } (\bar{X} - LSL)/3\,\sigma$$

The factor that is lowest is the controlling factor. If the process average is positioned exactly at the mid-tolerance dimension, the two values will be equal. A minimum value of 1.33 is commonly used to designate an ongoing process as meeting specification requirements.

The C_{pk} factor should also be used to determine the position of the process average in relation to the specification limit. This can be accomplished by examining the results of the calculation for the largest value. The larger the value, the closer to the center it is. If the C_{pk} value increases as improvements are made, the inherent variability of the process is being reduced or the engineering specification was changed to increase the tolerance.

$\overline{X}$-R Charts
Appendix 6B

How to Prepare $\overline{X}$-R Charts

Method:
1. Determine the parameter or parameters to be measured.
2. Determine the sample size to use. For $\overline{X}$-R charts, the sample size can be two to ten, but usually it is two to five. Once set, this sample size will be referred to as *n*. Note: Once the sample size of the group is set, it cannot vary from one sample to another. Different sample sizes can be used for different parameters, but the sample size must remain constant for any one parameter.
3. Determine the timing for taking the sample. Develop a form that includes a method for easily indicating the time, parameter measured, and quantity of parts to be measured.
4. Run the process as usual. Do not add or take away steps as data are being gathered. Obtain a series of groups of measurements, each group containing the *n* number of samples. Gather twenty or more groups, if possible, but not less than ten.
5. Compute the range for each group of data samples. This is referred to as *R*. The range is calculated by subtracting the lowest value in a group of data from the highest value.

6. After calculating the individual R values, calculate the average of the R values. This is referred to as $\bar{R}$ and represents the centerline for the R chart. Draw it as a solid horizontal line (see Figure 6.8).

7. Multiply $\bar{R}$ by D_4 and D_3 (see control-chart factors below) to obtain the upper and lower control limits for the R chart. Draw the control limits as dotted horizontal lines.

Control-Chart Factors

n*	A_2**	D_3***	D_4***	d_2
2	1.88	0	3.27	1.128
3	1.02	0	2.57	1.693
4	.73	0	2.28	2.059
5	.58	0	2.11	2.326
6	.48	0	2.00	2.534
7	.42	.08	1.92	
8	.37	.14	1.86	
9	.34	.18	1.82	
10	.31	.22	1.78	

*n is the sample size.
**A_2 is the factor for the $\bar{X}$ chart.
***D_3 and D_4 are factors for the R chart.

8. Using graph paper, establish an appropriate scale. For practical purposes, note that the upper and lower control limits of both the R and $\bar{X}$ chart should be approximately two inches apart.

9. Plot the successive values of R on this chart and connect the points with straight lines as in Figure 6.8.

10. Identify any points outside the control limits by marking an x at each out-of-control point.

R Control chart

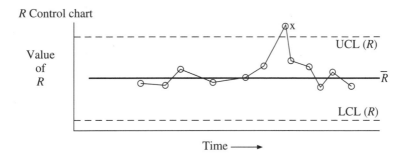

$\overline{X}$ Control chart

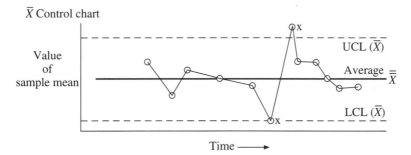

UCL = Upper Control Limit
LCL = Lower Control Limit

Note:
The data values marked "x" are statistically unreasonable and considered to be out of process control.

Figure 6.8   Statistical process control chart.

11. Interpret the chart (a job for a QC engineer), but it is best to wait until the $\overline{X}$ chart is done.

12. Proceed to the next level of analysis, using the same groups of measurements used for the R chart.

13. Calculate an average for each of the groups. This is referred to as $\overline{X}$. Next, calculate the average of the averages. This is referred to as $\overline{\overline{X}}$ and represents the centerline for the $\overline{X}$ chart. Draw it as a solid horizontal line.

14. Calculate the UCL and LCL for the $\overline{X}$ chart:

Upper control limit for $\overline{X}$ chart $= \overline{\overline{X}} + A_2 \times \overline{R}$

Lower control limit for $\overline{X}$ chart $= \overline{\overline{X}} - A_2 \times \overline{R}$

Draw the control limits as dotted horizontal lines on the $\overline{X}$ chart (see Figure 6.8).

15. Choose a scale for the $\overline{X}$ chart that is properly related to the scale already chosen for the R chart. The scale should be such that the distance between the control limits on the $\overline{X}$ chart is roughly similar to the distance between the control limits on the R chart.

16. After drawing the $\overline{X}$ chart, plot the data on the chart, remembering to enter the samples in their proper time sequence. Connect the points with a straight line. Mark an x on the chart where out-of-control conditions occur. As a matter of interest, draw the specification limits in the left-hand margin. Remember: In this $\overline{X}$ chart, averages are being plotted, not actual values as was done in the R chart. Therefore, the distribution of the actual values will be wider than the control limits on the $\overline{X}$ control chart.

17. Use a good text or work with a QC engineer to analyze your results for both the $\overline{X}$ and $\overline{R}$ charts. Take action based on the analysis.

Evidence of Conformance

Chapter 7

A purchasing organization's best strategy is to place the responsibility for quality and reliability on the supplier. This can be done by establishing performance requirements and reaching an understanding with the supplier that defective parts are not acceptable. The supplier needs to understand that defects will result in returned lots or, sometimes, returned parts with invoices for sorting costs, production time lost, or even penalties imposed by the end customer. The only approach is for the supplier to establish controls to ensure that parts meet requirements.

In some cases, procuring companies accept the task of determining whether the goods conform to the requirements of the purchase order. This may occur even if much of the responsibility for quality is delegated to the supplier. The importance of specifying requirements clearly and accurately has been established in earlier chapters. Both the supplier and the buyer should be in agreement as to exactly what is to be furnished.

The purchasing company must determine how to judge whether the goods conform to the requirements. Inspection can be performed at the supplier's plant prior to shipment, or it can be performed at the buyer's plant after receipt of goods. In some cases, techniques other than inspection are used. Still, both the supplier and user should realize that inspecting a product after it is produced adds no value to the product, and in some cases, inspection can even damage the part. Control of processes is required to ensure product conformance.

In some cases, verification of conformance might have to be done later, upon installation into the final product or even during use. It is best that all this be agreed upon by the supplier and buyer when the purchase order becomes final. Some advantages of each verification method are considered in the following paragraphs.

The amount of inspection also has to be established by the buyer. Engineering and quality control, working with the purchasing department, decide which characteristics to inspect or test and how many items are to undergo each check. The number of items to check depends on several factors. The importance of each characteristic must be considered. The cost of checking and difficulty of performing each inspection or test are also important considerations. If items could be destroyed or damaged by the test, this also creates a limitation. Sometimes the buyer does not have the necessary test or inspection equipment to perform all the checks upon receipt. Each of these factors is considered in planning for the inspection and testing for each type of item purchased from suppliers.

Especially careful or thorough inspection is needed under the following circumstances:

1. Considerable labor is to be subsequently expended on the item.
2. The item goes into an assembly, and the entire assembly will be lost or expensive rework will result if the item is found to be defective.
3. The item cannot be readily evaluated later, and eventual product function or salability will be affected.

4. Defectives may seriously affect manufacturing operations.
5. Safety of workers or of customers may be jeopardized by defectives.
6. Items cannot be returned for credit later because of the terms of the purchase order.

Inspection Upon Receipt of Goods

In just-in-time delivery, inspection upon receipt only has the advantage of determining if a disaster is about to occur. If material is being delivered as it is needed, there is no time to return anything. The only possible action is to sort or rework the goods as they are being used. Immediate action is then needed to ensure that the supplier will not deliver defective products in the future.

For example, when a purchase order has been given to a supplier, it is important to define the methods of inspection. When the goods arrive at the buyer's receiving dock, the exact procedures for testing and inspection can then be implemented without delay. Ideally, these inspection or test methods have been correlated with those of the supplier.

When received, the goods are identified and the quantity determined before inspection starts. It is necessary to have a copy of the purchase order at hand for use in establishing the applicable requirements. Sometimes shipments must be set aside until inspection or testing can begin. In some cases, a sample will be removed from the shipment and sent to a laboratory for testing which cannot be done by the receiving inspection; in other cases, each item is checked for certain characteristics. Often, a sample from the lot is inspected more extensively to establish the acceptability of the entire lot. When defects are found, liability for the defects must be determined. Obviously, the customer cannot hold the supplier responsible for nonconformances that the customer's employees or process caused.

Case Example. A customer rejected several lots of material due to a visual defect on the front of the part. The customer wanted to cancel the purchase order on the grounds of poor quality. The supplier investigated its process and some samples of the product about to be shipped. No defect could be found. The supplier visited the customer and reviewed the handling process. A step in the handling process was found to cause the damage. Correcting the process eliminated the defect. The supplier repaired the items at the customer's expense and returned the lots for use.

Prompt checking for conformance is important, since delays can impair the buyer's ability to reject a shipment. Delay in performing inspection can also cause production problems in cases where the items are needed to keep lines moving. Delays can also result in items accumulating and becoming mixed up or difficult to control. Control charts have been used effectively to identify excessive processing times or to address accusations that the quality control department unnecessarily delayed inspection. In the latter case, the charts may establish that the average inspection times are less than the delays on the receiving dock.

Responsibilities Upon Receipt of Goods

When the purchaser receives goods, responsibilities can be divided into two categories. One function, usually the responsibility of the quality control department, is to ascertain that the goods conform to the requirements. This function will be discussed in more detail in Chapter 8. The other function involves physical receipt, identification, and movement of goods to stores or to the place of next usage, as well as notification of appropriate internal company personnel. The notification to accounting may await inspection to assure conformance to the purchase order requirements before payment is made to the supplier. Ideally, if a supplier is properly selected and well developed, receiving inspection can and should be omitted. The supplier should be expected to provide good quality and react to any unacceptable conditions.

While the goods are in the receiving area, protection against pilferage and unauthorized use must be provided prior to completion of inspection. If goods are determined to be nonconforming, they must be segregated in a secure area to avoid inadvertent use.

Furthermore, the purchasing department should be notified promptly upon receipt of goods so that purchasing records will be updated to show that goods have been received. The proper identification of goods is important from the quality standpoint as well as for other reasons. For example, the received goods must be matched to the proper purchase order so that inspection personnel will know which requirements apply to each shipment. Any test data or other information furnished by the supplier with the shipment should be placed with the goods.

Finally, the receiving group (usually not quality control) should determine the quantity received. This information is also important to inspection personnel, since sample sizes to be inspected or tested depend upon the lot size received. In addition, the purchasing department needs to know the quantity received in order to determine whether the order is complete, since partial shipments are common. Sometimes the received material is identified only by the supplier's catalog description, and it must be further identified upon receipt to permit proper disposition and inspection. In many firms, this receipt and recording are accomplished with an on-line computer system, which also can be used to record quality information.

Results of Inspection and Tests

After tests or inspections have been completed on any lot or shipment of supplier's goods, a record or report is prepared. The record shows the inspections and tests conducted and the results. Sometimes the results are recorded on the purchase order or other standard record form. The quality control department should retain a copy of the results in case any repetitive problems arise in the future. Purchasing should also receive a copy of the results so that the supplier can be informed of any nonconformance found. Favorable results may be used to authorize payment to the supplier. The purchasing agent can do this by forwarding the authorization for payment to the accounting department.

If the test or inspection shows that the goods fail to comply with any requirements, one of two actions may result. Either the whole shipment can be returned to the supplier, or—if the discrepancy is minor—the buyer may consult with production, engineering, and quality control to determine if the items might be repaired or even used as they are. Some facilities have a material review board to establish this usability. This review may result in use of all or part of the items in the shipment. Any costs involved due to the nonconformities will have to be negotiated with the supplier. An urgent need for the items in production may provide a reason for not returning them to the supplier. In any case, corrective action must be taken to prevent suppliers from shipping additional items with the same problems.[1]

Alternatives for Handling Nonconforming Items
When all or part of a shipment received from a supplier does not conform to the quality standards or requirements, several alternatives are available to the buyer.

Always, however, the first action is to notify the supplier and request immediate evaluation of the problem and on-site corrective action resulting in good parts. Other actions, involve coordination and approval from other departments, such as engineering, quality control, and production—and sometimes from the customer of the final product. Of course, communication with the supplier concerning any contemplated action is essential. Comments or recommendations from personnel performing the inspection, which are made available with the test results, can often be very helpful in resolving problems. The buyer's final decision should take into account past quality history of

1. Richard T. Weber, *An Easy Approach to Acceptance Sampling: How to Use MIL-STD-105E.* (Milwaukee, Wis.: ASQC Quality Press, 1991).

the supplier and whether or not this same defect has occurred in previous shipments. The following alternatives are available.

Complete Rejection

The purchaser has the option of returning nonconforming goods to the supplier. This is usually the best alternative unless the defects are minor or some or all of the items are critically needed and can be made usable. Papers are prepared by the purchasing department to return the goods at the supplier's expense. The supplier should be notified prior to return, since sometimes the supplier may choose to have the defective goods disposed of or shipped to another destination rather than returned. The purchasing agent also must decide whether the supplier should send a replacement shipment of conforming goods or whether the order is being terminated due to default by the supplier. The agent may then procure the items elsewhere. The supplier's invoice will not be processed for payment. A supplier who has already been paid can be billed for the returned items. If replacement from the same supplier is expected, the return is documented in case there are any questions about shipments in the future.

Repair

With the concurrence of engineering and quality control, it may be feasible to repair the nonconforming items received from the supplier. In some cases, the supplier may elect to send representatives to the buyer's facility to make the repairs or modifications at the supplier's own expense. A supplier who makes such a repair is then fully aware of the discrepancy and the costs involved. If the buyer were to have company people perform the repairs, negotiations with the supplier to recover costs may result in differences of opinion. Also, when the supplier performs the repairs or modifications, the buyer later can reject the items if they still are not satisfactory. If the buyer handles the repairs, the supplier may contend that any problems turning up later are a result if the repair work done by the buyer's personnel. In either case, the buyer may seek a price reduction for the repaired goods.

Several other actions are important when nonconforming supplier's goods are found. First, the purchasing agent must consult with the other departments involved in the decision. Second, the supplier must be made aware of the rejection promptly. Finally, all returns or other actions must be documented for records and control and for use in keeping track of supplier-quality histories. This approach will best satisfy both the business needs and quality needs of the buyer's company.

Use "As Is"

If the defects are minor, the purchasing agent may secure approval of engineering and quality control to use the material "as is." The supplier should still be made aware of the nonconformance and the fact that it could have been rejected. The shipment should still go on the supplier's record as not conforming to the requirements.

Partial Rejection

The buyer, with approval from engineering and quality control, may decide to reject a portion of the shipment. The part retained may be used "as is" or repaired, depending on the defect. The lot would still be considered as nonconforming for supplier-rating purposes.

Rework

Rework means returning defective items to specification requirements with no deviations. This should mean that MRB action is not required except to

1. verify that the rework cured the deviation and will not affect reliability,
2. provide traceability so that field failures can be traced to the rework action, and
3. ensure that corrective action is taken to prevent further occurrences.

Businesses do not want to depend on rework because it obviously takes effort beyond what has been planned and causes schedules to be missed.

Nonconforming Goods—Legal Aspects

When receiving goods from a supplier, the contractor goes through some type of inspection or test to determine if the goods are acceptable. The UCC says that acceptance cannot occur until the buyer has had a reasonable chance to inspect the goods. The inspections may or may not check for all requirements. On the basis of these checks, however, the contractor may determine that the goods do not conform to one or more of the requirements.

Whichever action is selected, further remedies are available. For example, the contractor could accept four items from the nonconforming lot, send the remaining twenty back to the supplier, and still sue the supplier for breach of contract. A company might take that action if it badly needed the four items and was able to repair them to make them usable. The company might then sue for the repair costs and also damages suffered because conforming items were not available. However, any action taken by the procuring company must be in good faith. For example, goods no longer needed should not be sent back claiming they are defective if they are good.

Note also that the UCC refers to units. For example, if the purchase order was for fifty drums of oil, the contractor would not be justified in accepting part of a drum. In any dispute, the purchase order will be consulted to ascertain what constitutes a unit. Thus, it would be wise for any inspection or sampling plans to be consistent with the units expressed in the purchase order. This is another important reason why quality control personnel should work with the buyer before the purchase order is placed. The best way to avoid any controversy, however, is for the supplier and contractor to agree on all terms of the contract and also on the procedure for inspection as part of the terms of the purchase order.

If receiving inspection finds the lots to be nonconforming, does that constitute rejection? An acceptance or rejection becomes effective only when the supplier is notified. In the notification, the buyer must clearly state the defect found. At that time, the supplier can make disposition of the rejected lot. The supplier may repair the defect or find another customer who can use the nonconforming goods. This means that the buyer may not be able to change his or her mind and accept the shipment after rejecting it and notifying the supplier of the rejection.

For the buyer to preserve rights, any rejection or acceptance must be clear and timely. Continued silence on the part of the buyer may constitute acceptance after a reasonable time. If there is a rejection, it then becomes the supplier's responsibility to specify disposition of the rejected goods within a reasonable period of time. Very often the buyer's use of the goods can be considered acceptance unless there has been clear communication to the supplier specifying otherwise. Much depends on the contract language and the written communications by the two parties.

In one case that came to court, the buyer purchased production equipment to be installed in a facility operated by a lessee. The contract stated that the buyer's obligation to pay was conditional on the satisfaction of the lessee. When the goods arrived, the lessee notified the supplier that the equipment was unsatisfactory and asked that it be removed. A supplier's representative visited the plant and made some adjustments. The representative later testified that the equipment was in use and working properly when he left the plant.

After the first production run, the supplier was again notified of defects. More adjustments followed, but the lessee couldn't get a satisfactory production run and stopped using the equipment. When the supplier sued for price, the buyer pleaded that there was no acceptance of the goods. The trial court ruled for the supplier, but the buyer appealed. The appellate court found no evidence that the lessee had signified the equipment as conforming or had agreed to retain it despite its nonconformity.

In another case, the contract specified that the goods were to be picked up at the supplier's plant. The supplier notified the buyer that they were ready, but the buyer neither picked them up nor rejected them. In the lawsuit, the buyer pointed out that by terms of the contract, title did not pass until the items were paid for. The court held that title was independent of acceptance—and the buyer had accepted the goods because he had not rejected them.

Revoking Acceptance

What if the buyer accepts a shipment of goods and then changes his or her mind? Again, the contract terms must define the point of acceptance. Any preliminary or conditional acceptance should be stated as such. The UCC gives protection to the seller, and when the buyer accepts in accordance with the terms of the purchase order, a subsequent rejection will not usually be enforceable. The UCC does, however, allow revocation of an acceptance under certain conditions as follows:

1. The goods do not conform to the specified requirements.
2. The value to the buyer of the supplier's goods is reduced substantially due to a nonconformance.
3. It was difficult to determine the nonconformance.
4. The supplier provided assurance that the requirements were met.
5. The buyer had reason to assume that the supplier was going to correct the nonconformance.

In any of these situations, the buyer must notify the supplier within a reasonable time after the nonconformity is discovered. Also, the revocation must be made before there is any substantial change in the goods not caused by their original defects.

On some occasions, a supplier will agree to a purchase order specifying that the buyer must be satisfied with the goods. In other words, even though the goods conform to the requirements, the supplier has agreed to allow the buyer to return them. A court will uphold the buyer's right to return goods in these cases, but the buyer has the burden to prove that the terms are in the agreement.

Quality control engineers and inspectors should have an understanding of these legal aspects of the UCC to carry out inspection responsibilities in a way that does not jeopardize the rights or assets of the company. The UCC provides that the receiving company's rejection must be within a reasonable time after delivery. Again, the term *rejection* includes notification to the supplier, but does not require the buyer to return the goods, even if the buyer had indicated that they would be returned. Once the goods are rejected, it is the supplier's responsibility to take action for their disposition. If the buyer does not reject and notify the supplier within a reasonable time, the right to do so later may be forfeited. This is true unless acceptance or rejection is at a later point—such as after assembly into a product where the fit can be verified. This again emphasizes the need for close coordination between quality personnel and purchasing personnel as the decisions to reject or accept are made and disposition of material is established.

Supplier-Furnished Data

It is the responsibility of the purchasing department to procure items meeting their company's quality standards and requirements. This includes the responsibility to ensure that quality requirements are met without excessive cost. In many cases, these objectives can be best achieved if the supplier sends the test results along with the goods. Although these data may not be used as the sole basis for acceptance by the buyer, they are often of considerable value. In some instances, receiving inspection may verify the supplier's data on a spot-check basis. In other cases, receiving inspection may compare its inspection results with the supplier's data. If there are any differences, the data serve as a base from which to work with the supplier and more quickly establish reasons for the difference.

In some cases, the supplier may use process-control charts to ensure quality. Process control charts and their interpretation are covered in Chapter 6. Copies of such charts might be sent along with the shipment by the supplier as evidence that the goods conform to the requirements. In other cases, C_{pk} values calculated from data are provided to demonstrate control of part and process (see Chapter 6, Appendix 6A). Process-control charts would be applicable to chemicals, wire, yarn, or other materials manufactured in a continuous process. The buyer might still, however, check a sample upon receipt of the shipment. The practice of requiring the supplier to send actual test results or other data provides much greater assurance to the buyer than merely asking for a certificate stating that all requirements are met. In addition, the data can be used by the buyer's quality control or engineering personnel for evaluation or to help resolve any problems that occur later in assembly or after shipment of the final product.

Effective Use of Supplier's Quality Data

The procuring company can achieve both cost savings and added quality assurance through the systematic use of supplier-supplied data. Initially, the supplier furnishes the test or inspection data with each shipment. If only a sample is checked by the supplier, the sampled material might be packed separately from the rest of the lot. The buyer can then perform similar tests or inspections on the same sample and compare results with those furnished by the supplier. If there are differences, they must be investigated and resolved, but this can be accomplished faster if both parties have checked the same items.

As the buyer develops confidence in the supplier's ability to control processes, hold tolerances, and perform tests, the amount of checking performed by the buyer can be reduced. The buyer can rely more on the supplier and perform spot checks on a monitoring basis. If any discrepancies do turn up, it may be necessary to reinstitute more inspection as well as to require corrective action from the supplier. In general, the use of supplier-furnished data provides both cost savings and further assurance of quality conformance.

Inspection at Source

Inspection by the buyer at the supplier's plant prior to shipment is called *source inspection*, or supplier surveillance. Sometimes source inspection involves actual inspection, in which the buyer sends inspectors to the supplier's plant to perform the inspection. In other instances, the buyer's representative may witness the supplier's tests or ask for data showing test results. There are several reasons for using source inspection.

1. The inspection equipment is not available at the buyer's facility, either due to its high cost or for other reasons.
2. The purchase order specifies acceptance at the supplier's facility.
3. Inspection or tests can best be performed during manufacture, such as by use of process-control charts.
4. The parties wish to avoid the costs of returning shipments, especially if the goods are costly to ship, the shipping distance is great, or the schedule would not tolerate a delay.
5. The goods are to be shipped directly to the using customer or to a field-use site without going to the buyer's facility.
6. There have been frequent quality problems in the past.
7. The parties have a cost-plus contract, and the buyer logically wants to help the supplier prevent the production of nonconforming items.
8. The buyer does not have trained personnel to perform the tests or inspection.

The policy of inspecting at source is widely used by the Department of Defense and by other contractors when one or more of these factors are present.

For source inspection to be successful, the buyer must delegate authority to the personnel performing the source inspection. These source inspectors may need training in inspection and testing, and they also should have knowledge of the function of the supplied items and the final products using the items. In some cases, the source inspection personnel may need to communicate with technical people back at the buyer's plant to resolve any technical questions before the final acceptance at source is authorized. Any delay resulting from difficulties in communication can make source inspection less desirable.

The quantity of items ordered and the value of goods purchased must also be sufficient to justify keeping the buyer's inspectors at the supplier's facility on a continuing basis. One alternative is to have the supplier notify the buyer when the goods are ready to be inspected so that someone can then be sent to the supplier's facility.

The costs of inspection should be considered as part of the costs of the supplied material. If source inspection is to be required, the buyer may need to consider distance from its plant as a factor when suppliers are being evaluated. If several types of items are being procured from the same supplier, or from suppliers in the same location, costs of source inspection may be reduced. An *itinerant inspector* is one who drops in at a supplier's plant occasionally. The inspector may have the responsibility for inspection of several suppliers in a general area. This contrasts with the function of the resident inspector, who resides permanently at the supplier's facility. In some cases, resident quality control or test engineers must be used to monitor complex products and testing prior to shipment. This is true more often for complex equipment.

Duties of the Source Inspector

Responsibilities will be assigned to the source inspection personnel based on the nature of the product, past quality history, and the nature of the specified requirements. The following are examples of activities that may be assigned to source inspection personnel:

1. First-piece inspection or monitoring of final tests performed by the supplier in accordance with the specification
2. Checking test or inspection data or reports, and possibly signing off on each report if the test was witnessed
3. Keeping buyer's purchasing department advised of possible delays due to schedule delays or quality problems at the supplier's facility, providing early warnings of possible technical problems that might occur after delivery
4. Ensuring that failed items or failure reports returned to the supplier are properly followed up to determine causes of

the failure, ensuring that corrective action is taken by supplier to prevent further failures

5. Monitoring the supplier's quality control system and procedures to make sure they are being followed

6. Participating in the review of nonconforming items being considered for use (handled by a material review board in some facilities), acting for the buyer, and coordinating with people back at the plant where necessary

7. Monitoring qualification tests performed at the supplier's facility

8. Monitoring in-process quality controls used in manufacture

9. Ascertaining that design changes are approved and incorporated at the proper time as specified by the purchase order

10. Accepting goods at the supplier plant for the buyer when authorized to do so, rejecting material that does not conform

11. Informing supplier's and buyer's management of problems

Persons performing source inspection should be selected on the basis not only of technical competence, but also of ability to deal effectively with supplier personnel. They must understand their responsibilities as agents of the buyer as well as the limitations on their activities. It is usually desirable to transfer source inspection personnel periodically so that personal relationships do not become too close.

Surveillance of the Supplier's Operations

As part of source inspection, the buyer's representative should look at the supplier's overall operations. The following are some guidelines for doing this:

1. Make sure that quality objectives are in agreement with supplier's company objectives.

2. Check to see whether the quality control people work with and motivate people in other parts of the supplier's organization.

3. Determine whether preventive activities are taken by quality control before production starts.
4. Does the supplier have a continuous evaluation of products and activities?
5. Does the supplier have well-defined standards for all products?
6. Are corrective actions taken when rejections occur, in order to prevent further occurrence of the problems?
7. Does the supplier have a good data-collection and record system? When defects recur, the records are needed.

Process Controls

The source inspector often has the responsibility for surveillance of the supplier's processes. Statistical techniques can be applied to matching operations or other repetitive processes. Some basic concepts that would be helpful in source-inspection tasks are illustrated here.

Variation

Items manufactured in a machining or other manufacturing process are not all exactly alike. Each measurable dimension will vary to some extent on either side of the nominal value. Usually the variation is in the form of a normal curve. Since these variations are very small (perhaps as small as a few thousandths of a centimeter), the parts may appear to the naked eye to be identical. Precision gages or test equipment, however, can show the differences. An objective of a quality control system is to control variation so the specified tolerances are not exceeded.

Variation occurs in three different ways. A particular dimension can differ slightly from one item to the next. We will call this the *item-to-item variation*. There can also be variation in a particular characteristic within a piece. For example, diameter may vary along the length of the rod. The third type of variation can occur over time. As a tool wears from usage, for example, a resulting machined dimension may become greater.

Variation can result from a variety of causes. The first possible cause is the process itself, such as the machine and tool. The raw material can also vary and cause variation in the product. People are the cause of the third possible variation, such as variation due to the operator of the machine. Other factors such as temperature or humidity can also cause variation in a dimension.

Any process has some inherent variation due to chance. Other variation is due to an *assignable cause*, such as an incorrect setting or tool wear. It is an objective of quality control to identify when an assignable cause exists so that a process can be corrected. This requires the separation of the assignable causes from the chance causes of variation, since the chance causes are expected.

Process-Control Charts

As we discussed in Chapter 6, a control chart provides a graphic presentation of the variation in a process. The typical process-control chart plots readings as a particular dimension or other characteristics being measured. The diameter of a machined part is an example of a dimension that could be plotted. A control chart for the diameter of a part is illustrated in Figure 7.1.

In this particular chart, a sample of five parts is taken each hour, where the production rate is approximately one hundred parts per hour. The diameters of the five parts are measured, and the sample mean of the five is calculated and plotted on the chart. If the variation

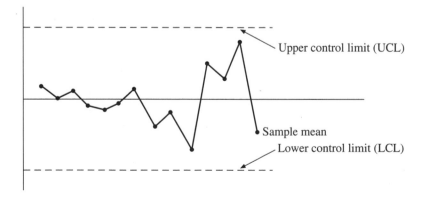

Figure 7.1   Process-control chart.

exceeds the upper (UCL) or lower (LCL) limit, it is greater than that due to chance alone. If either limit is exceeded, the operation is stopped until the cause of the excessive variation is determined. In the case illustrated, a tool had become loose and was reset.

While there are several types of control charts, some of which plot values other than the mean value, the principle of stopping the process if the limit is exceeded always applies.

Examine each of the process control charts in Figure 7.2. Assume that you observe each one in a supplier's process. Answer the following for each chart:

1. Is an assignable cause present?
2. Would you recommend that the process be stopped?
3. What is a possible cause of the problem, if one exists?
4. Can you make any suggestions?

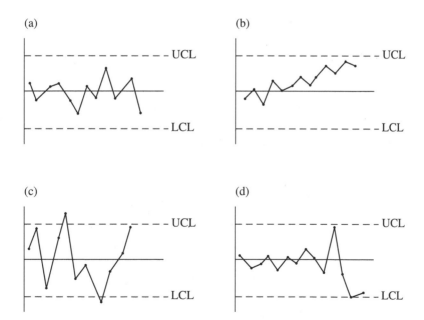

Figure 7.2   Analyzing process-control charts.

Chart (a) shows a process that is in control. In chart (b), although the limit has not been exceeded, it appears that it soon will be, due to the continuous trend. The process should be stopped immediately before any defective items are produced. Since the trend is gradual, tool wear is a possible cause. The tool could be set between the central line and the LCL. This would be better than resetting to the central line, since a reset to below the central line will allow more wear before measurements again become close to the UCL. Chart (c) indicates that both control limits have been exceeded. There are no trends. A loose tool could cause this type of situation. The process should have been stopped when the upper control limit was first exceeded. In chart (d), the first ten points plotted on the chart stayed close to the central line. Although neither limit has been exceeded, the sudden increase in variation should arouse concern and be investigated.

Lot Plot

When the parts being produced by a machine are measured and the measurements recorded in a plot as pictured in Figure 7.3, we call this a *lot plot*. The lot plot can tell us how capable the machine is of holding the tolerance needed to stay within specified limits, whether the machine is set properly, and whether something appears to be causing the measurements to be out of control. In Figure 7.3, it appears that the machine has the ability to hold to the specification

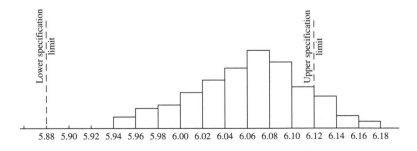

Figure 7.3   Lot plot.

limits of 5.88 to 6.12, but that it is set so that the nominal falls on 6.06 rather than 6.00.

Normal Distribution

Most machines and processes yield dimensions or other characteristics in the form of a normal curve as shown in Figure 7.4. If a machine were set to turn a shaft of 6 cm in diameter, we know that all shafts would not be exactly the same. The precision of the machine would determine how close the variation could be held. From past experience, we might know that the parts would fall in a distribution as pictured with *almost* 100 percent of the items being within ± .120 cm of the mean value at which the machine is set.

Normal-curve theory actually establishes that 99.7 percent of the parts will fall within three standard deviations of the mean. In the case pictured, three standard deviations equal .120, and one standard deviation would be .040, or one-third of .120.

Tolerances

If a drawing specified 6.00 ± .24 cm, the tolerance would be .24 cm in either direction from the nominal value. The machine could easily hold this tolerance if set at the nominal (6.00). If the drawing specified 6.00 ± .09 cm, the limited natural capability of the machine could

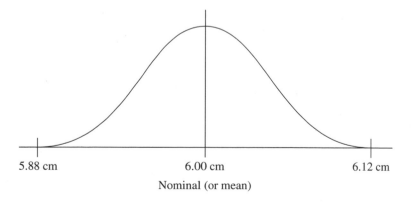

| 5.88 cm | 6.00 cm | 6.12 cm |

Nominal (or mean)

Figure 7.4   Normal curve.

prevent it from holding all parts produced within the tolerance. It would be necessary, then, to select a better machine that could hold a tighter tolerance.

Examples for Analysis
Each of the lot plots in Figure 7.5 was made from a sample of fifty items. Assume that each sample of fifty was taken from a different lot of material received from the supplier. Make a preliminary analysis of each lot plot based on your observation. Specification limits are shown by *S*.

Possible evaluations of each lot plot are given below:

a. This plot can be expected from a normal distribution process with all parts within the specification limit.
b. The process would be able to hold the specification limits if the nominal were set to the right.
c. The machine or process has too much natural variation and—although it appears normal—points on both ends of the distribution are out of the specified limits.
d. It appears that the process was not set on the correct nominal and that parts not within limits were removed from the lot after it was produced.
e. Same as (d), except that the gage used in sorting was not set correctly and defectives are present.
f. Same as (e), except the gage was set in a way that rejected some good items.
g. It appears that parts from two different lots have been mixed together. One lot does not meet the requirements.

Case Example. A company was planning to procure item "X," where a diameter was critical and particularly difficult to machine. Two suppliers each claimed to be able to meet the requirement. The buyer ordered five hundred parts from

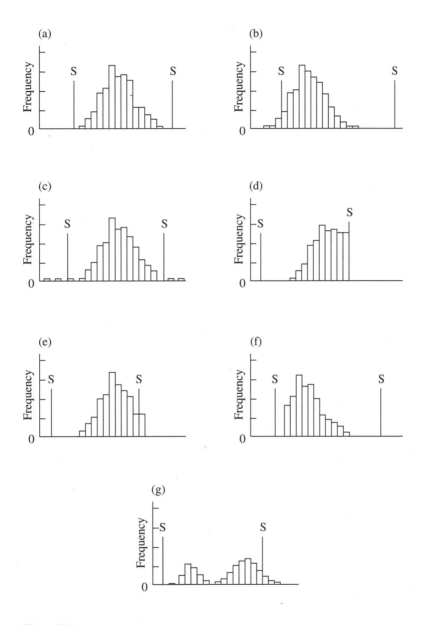

Figure 7.5   Analyzing lot plots.

each supplier as a trial to determine ability to meet the specification requirement. Upon receipt, the items from each supplier were carefully inspected and were within specified tolerance. The buyer then had the measurements of each supplier recorded in a lot plot as shown in Figure 7.6. From the lot plots, he concluded that Supplier A produced five hundred items, all within specifications, by a controlled process. He also concluded that Supplier B sorted out and submitted five hundred items within the limits. It was apparent to the buyer that if orders were given to B, costly 100 percent inspection would be required, and some out-of-tolerance items might get shipped. Supplier A, however, seemed able to produce all good items under a controlled process, and should be given the order.

Case Example. A supplier's part was an integral part of a complex electromechanical assembly. Once assembled, removal of the supplier's part would require ten hours for complete disassembly and five hours for reassembly. Five percent of the end products were being found defective as a result of this one supplier part. With production volume of 1500 units per day, this meant that 75 units were being rejected each day. Sampling at receiving inspection required about 1.5 hours per item, and the sample size and acceptable quality level (AQL) being used would allow 5 percent defective items to be accepted. Efforts with the supplier con-

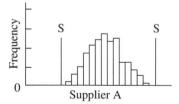
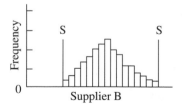

Figure 7.6 Comparing two suppliers.

sisted of the supplier verifying the defective condition fewer than 20 percent of the time.

Production engineering and quality engineering identified an easily measurable characteristic that indicated the status of an actual process parameter. By luck, the characteristic had been measured and recorded along with the serial number at receiving inspection for a three-month period. Since each part's serial number indicated date and sequence, it was possible to place the incoming data in the order in which the parts were produced. A sample of five successive data values were averaged, and a range was calculated for each four-hour manufacturing period.

Using this data, an $\overline{X}$-R chart was drawn (see Chapter 6, Appendix 6B). The results are shown in Figure 7.7. The $\overline{X}$ chart showed that every 6 to 8 days the process went out of control and then made a radical improvement. The range chart, however, stayed within the control limits.

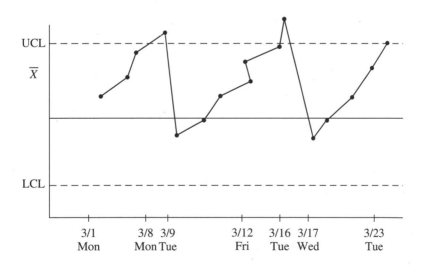

Time in days (or sample no.)

Figure 7.7 $\overline{X}$ chart for case example.

Investigation by the supplier showed that the condition occurred concurrently with planned, periodic, preventive maintenance activities. Performing maintenance at shorter intervals eliminated the out-of-control condition and the rejection.

Inspection and Testing

Chapter 8

T he function of quality control can be separated into two tasks: *control of quality* (defect prevention) and *verification of quality*. Inspection and testing have traditionally fallen into the second category. Verification implies that inspection or testing must be performed to measure one or more characteristics of a product. In this chapter, we deal with inspection and testing as they apply to supplier-furnished products, materials, and services.

In formulating strategy, one question that a business must answer is whether to perform incoming inspection or, perhaps more realistically, when (how often or on which suppliers) to perform incoming inspection. Although this sounds like a simple decision, it is actually quite complex and carries with it an attitude that shapes a business's total approach to supplier quality.

A decision to perform incoming inspection implies that management is not placing the responsibility for quality fully on its purchasing organization and the supplier. Further, it shows management's acceptance that production delays will occur due to rejected lots. Finally, it places responsibility for business quality performance with a receiving inspector.

Why is this the case? Examine the questions that arise when a problem occurs with a supplier's part in the production environment of a company that has receiving inspection. Why didn't receiving inspection find the defect? Why wasn't the inspector trained better? Why doesn't quality control sort the parts? These are really the wrong questions to be asking. Instead, the question should be directed to the buyer and anyone involved with developing and selecting the supplier. Why didn't the supplier make the part correctly? Were the requirements properly transmitted to the supplier? What will the supplier do to maintain production on schedule?

Generally, when a business decides to perform receiving inspection, it rarely allocates sufficient resources to accomplish the expected task. The proper tools, personnel, and support are normally not in place. Controlling supplier quality through incoming inspection is a difficult task. If the decision is made to perform receiving inspection, then management support is required from a personnel, equipment, and facility standpoint. Some practical aspects of incoming inspection follow.

Planning for Incoming Inspection and Test

For each item to be purchased, someone must decide what type of person—possessing what skills and using what equipment—is necessary to verify that the item is satisfactory. This inspection or test can be performed at the supplier's or at the buyer's facility.

In conjunction with this decision, someone must also decide at what level or combination of levels to make inspections and tests. They can be performed on parts, assemblies, completed product, or combination of products assembled into a system. The decision of what and when to test is a matter of both economics and technical feasibility. Usually it is desirable to make inspections or tests as early as possible, preferably as the item is being manufactured. This permits making corrections to a process whenever there is evidence that the process is not in control. Sometimes, however, a characteristic cannot be measured until items are assembled together into components or assemblies. Normally we prefer to avoid having to dismantle components or assemblies to remove and replace defective items. Much production and assembly work can be automated, but rework and repair must be handled on an individual basis and, therefore, become costly. Thus, it is best to locate defectives at the earliest possible point.

Investigating the Product

Upon receipt of a shipment, little information is available to the inspector concerning how a supplier part was fabricated, so the inspection described previously requires some advance planning. The quality planner must recognize the pitfalls and provide ease of inspection as well as protection to the user. To achieve a satisfactory degree of protection against defects, the planner must investigate the part thoroughly. To simplify the approach, basic inspection concepts can be categorized by commodity types. For example, categories might include printed circuit boards, hardware, stampings, castings, turned parts, chemicals, software, and processes. If aligned with the purchasing department's breakdown of products, the planning can be done during initial contact with the supplier. This basic planning includes identification of the characteristics critical to the function of the product.

While investigating a part in the development of the inspection plan, a knowledge of the supplier's manufacturing technique and familiarity with the strengths or weaknesses of the manufacturing approach are helpful. For example, knowing that flash and "knit" lines in plastic moldings indicate potentially out-of-control conditions on tooling temperature or pressure would assist in developing a good plan. Knowing that a supplier has several machines producing the same part becomes a basis for developing the correct sample sizes or sampling approach. This knowledge should also be used to establish requirements for the supplier with respect to segregation and identification of material. If parts are properly segregated, stratified sampling or sampling by production machine or tool cavity can be accomplished.

Establishing a checklist that can be used in inspection or testing can ensure that the plan is effective. The checklist should cover the following questions:

- What method is used to produce the item?
  - ☐ Is the method prone to error?
  - ☐ Is the method variable?
  - ☐ Are there visual or easily measured values that can be used in verification?
  - ☐ Does each characteristic need to be measure?

- How many machines are producing the part?

- Is the tooling permanent?

- Is there more than one cavity?

- Are there secondary operations?
  - ☐ Any holes requiring tapping?
  - ☐ Any surfaces needing buffing?

- Is the process active, and does it require continuous attention to maintain stability?
  - ☐ When are additions made?
  - ☐ How are additions specified?
  - ☐ What method is used to verify additions?

- How can software be tested?
  - ☐ What system changes need to be anticipated?

- How can a random sample be selected?

- Can the characteristic be measured automatically or with instrumentation?

- How is supplied item used?

- How many are used in each assembly?

- What impact will a defect have?
    - ☐ Will the defect be detectable during use of part?
    - ☐ Will the defect be detectable during subsequent application in the product?
    - ☐ Will the defect be detectable prior to providing the end product to the customer?
    - ☐ What is the cost for rework of a defect?
    - ☐ Can the defect be reworked or will it result in scrap?
    - ☐ What impact will the defect have on production flow?
    - ☐ How will the defect affect the reliability and function of product?

- Will the sampling plan provide the needed protection?

- How many parts are received per lot?

- How often are lots received?

Sampling plans are often ineffective as a way of identifying defects that can have a serious impact on production flows. For example, if a product uses one hundred devices in each product, and the devices are received with a defect level of 1 percent, it is likely that on the average, every product in flow will have at least one defective device in it. Further, if the devices are inspected using a 1.5 percent AQL, the material will most likely always be accepted. Obviously, this is a special situation requiring evaluation and resolution, but it illustrates an important point.

After establishing answers to the checklist of questions above, an appropriate plan can be developed. The analysis may demonstrate the need to inspect one supplier's product differently than another's. If this is the case, the plan should clearly indicate how this is to be accomplished. Revisions to the plan can be easily made and incorporated based on either good or bad product performance. If the product performs well, reduced inspection might be allowed. If a defect is found, revision of inspection criteria must be promptly made.

Once completed, the inspection plan should be evaluated with an incoming lot to determine how well it works, both as to effectiveness and practicality. An inspection plan calling for a 1.5 percent AQL on all dimensions of a part having two hundred separate characteristics could easily require sixteen to twenty hours per part, and the better part of a month to do the complete lot. Unless the personnel are provided for this type of inspection, an alternate method must be developed.

The individual preparing an inspection plan should be required to perform the inspection on the first two or three lots of material. This will ensure that he or she understands the feasibility of accomplishing the plan and will also assist with determining whether any items have been missed.

Testing

Whether we are dealing with parts, components, assemblies, or entire systems, the purpose of a test is to ascertain whether the item functions as required in the specified environment. To accomplish the purpose, the person responsible for planning the testing must have a complete understanding of the item to be tested—its function, how it is to be used, and the environment in which it is to function. Every item will require tests that are unique to it. However, certain tests are traditional for items falling into a generic grouping.

Generic Tests

Certain tests can be applied to many types of products using general testing equipment. For example, a product may need to operate under certain temperature conditions. The temperature range may vary from item to item, but a standard environmental test chamber can be used to conduct the tests.

Generic tests can be grouped as follows:

1. Environmental—Testing under the temperature, humidity, pressure, vibration, or shock conditions a part is expected to endure in shipment, storage, and actual use
2. Acoustic or electromagnetic conditions

3. Reliability—Testing to determine if the product operates over a period of time without failure
4. Safety—Testing to verify that the user will not be injured while the product is in use or is being placed in service

Unique Tests

Certain tests are performed to verify characteristics peculiar to the product. These tests can be grouped as follows:

1. Functional—Testing to determine if the item performs as required
2. Maintainability—Testing to determine if the product can be serviced or repaired readily using available documentation and tools
3. Appearance factors and product identification markings
4. Physical measurements

Difficulties in Receiving Inspection

Inspection of a product at receiving is one of the most difficult tasks. Little information is available to indicate the critical factors to inspect. It's obviously too late for in-process checks. Moreover, more than one lot of raw material or more than one machine's output may be represented by a particular lot. Material fabricated or produced at different times may also be included in a lot. Furthermore, the product may be packaged to protect it from handling damage or the environment and may be bulky, heavy, or messy. In sum, any number of conditions may exist to present an inspector with difficulties. Yet the receiving inspector's responsibility is to ensure that defective material is rejected, that acceptable material is accepted, and that every possible interpretation of the requirements are known, understood, and applied. Regardless of the situation, accepting rejectable material and rejecting acceptable material are costly to both the supplier and user in terms of schedules, personnel, and profit margins. Neither error can be allowed to occur often without resulting in serious problems.

Commodity Similarities
Physical characteristics can restrain effective inspection. The material may be delivered in a train tank car or tractor trailer, or it may be corrosive, explosive, or temperature-sensitive. Or it could be so tiny as to require high magnification to see. In each case, a method of handling and processing material must be developed to assure an effective inspection. One approach is to establish guidelines for receiving inspection consistent with the type of commodity involved. In general, inspection approaches are similar for a commodity grouping. A typical commodity listing could include the following:

> raw chemicals
> steel
> precious metals
> hardware (screws, nuts, bolts)
> printed circuit boards
> electronic components (resistors, diodes, microchips)
> electronic assemblies
> software (programs)
> die-cast parts
> sheet metal
> painted parts
> motors
> transformers

Each of these groups could have generic inspection criteria. For instance, the generic requirements for a printed circuit board would be part number, outline (physical size, thickness, shape), hole size, no bridging of conductors, no breaks of conductors, proper plating thickness of contracts, adhesion of markings, location of holes on center (critical for automatic insertion), conductivity of the surface, and solderability. Using the characteristics described, an inspector can perform inspection on received material, and only selected special checks would need to be done to individual lots. However, the inspector should have written instructions detailing special characteristics to be checked on each lot.

Each commodity could easily have a list of characteristics identifying general requirements applying to each lot of material received, thereby maximizing the efficiency of control and minimizing the risk of accepting poor material.

Part Number Verification

Of all the inspections accomplished at receiving inspection, the verifying of proper part numbers is most common. This allows control of the material in the production system. If done incorrectly, material will be accepted that is incorrectly identified and can cause trouble later in production. If a part is accepted under the wrong number, it can result in false inventory records that will not support production requirements. It could also result in the mixing of stock, incorrect assemblies, rework, and scrap. Performing electrical and physical inspection might be the only way to verify the correct number for a part, but in any case, it must be done accurately.

Appearance

Inspecting a product for appearance is a function likely to cause difficulties between the supplier and user. Acceptability of appearance depends on the judgment of the inspector. For example, parts are often plated with nickel to provide protection and wear characteristics, yet nickel-plated items are often rejected because of poor appearance. The rejections seem to be proportioned to the lack of shine. Also, if raw material lines show through, the rejections increase. The more inspection an item receives, the more likely that appearance rejections will occur. Careful control of visual rejections is necessary, since the rejections may actually be uncalled for, or they may mask an incomplete inspection activity. Caution must be taken to assure that an appearance rejection, which quite often is the first characteristic to be inspected, does not preclude completion of the remainder of the inspection.

In the case of nickel-plated parts, appearance can be difficult to evaluate. Zinc chromate, if used as a substitute plating, will not cause as many appearance problems since it is nonuniform in appearance and color. It might be easier to change the plating material than to train everyone about the appearance criteria.

If the product requires certain appearance characteristics—such as a home appliance—then the criteria for acceptance or rejection should be clear, easy to interpret, and easily communicated. Often physical samples of acceptable and unacceptable appearance are needed to describe the characteristics. Such physical samples must be protected, since handling will affect the samples' appearance and result in a criteria change or invalidation of the inspection.

In some instances, acceptance standards are set by a group of typical samples, some acceptable and some unacceptable. This method is used, for example, in the beverage and food industry, where experts establish the appearance, taste, and appeal.

Physical Constraints
In many cases, physical constraints prevent or hamper an effective inspection. Sometimes train car or tractor trailer shipments of parts present difficulties in ensuring that a random sample is taken. What inspector is not tempted to sample the parts immediately available rather than go through the procedure of taking a random sample? The best alternative might be to inspect parts randomly as they are being moved from the conveying vehicle into the stockroom or to the production line. This system requires good control, since rejection of a lot entails capturing the complete lot and holding it in an appropriate location to allow return to the supplier or other disposition.

Where to Inspect and How Much Inspection

Where is the best inspection location from an economic perspective and what constitutes the legal acceptance of a shipment? The following are guidelines on where inspections (or tests) should be performed. In addition, these guidelines can be used to help determine the appropriate amount of inspection or testing upon receipt of goods from suppliers.

1. Inspect or test after operations with low yields so that more costly operations are not later run with defective products.

2. Inspect or test before operations in which relatively high value is added so that defectives are removed before further value is added.
3. Inspect or test before operations that may cover up defects or make defects difficult to find or to repair.
4. Inspect or test at points in the process when it is comparatively inexpensive, such as when the use of automatic test equipment is possible.

In any case, inspect or test in such a way that the results can be used to control quality and to prevent further defects. We can apply some of these concepts to determine the amount of inspection or testing to be performed upon receipt of the product by considering the next step in the process. To some extent, the discussion of *how much* inspection to perform is really a determination of *where* to inspect.

Amount of Incoming Inspection

Several studies have dealt with the amount of incoming inspection that is economically optimal. Even with a great number of variables, we can identify some rules of thumb. Generally, there are three choices: (1) no incoming inspection, (2) 100 percent inspection, or (3) acceptance sampling.

Throughout this book we have taken the position that the preferred strategy is to ensure that supplied goods are free of defects— and in many cases this actually is a feasible strategy. The second alternative is 100 percent inspection upon receipt. Although human error prevents this method from being perfect, we may achieve 100 percent effective inspection or testing with automatic testing equipment. If we use acceptance sampling, the implication is that a certain percentage of defects is acceptable, and the buyer will probably get that percentage in the supplied goods.

With these thoughts in mind, a company may decide it wants to receive 100 percent good items. However, that goal is not always attainable. The question then is, should 100 percent testing be performed upon receipt, or should no testing be performed and failed items be removed and replaced later in the assembled product? To respond to this question, where the objective is to perform the economically optimal action, some rough rules of thumb are helpful. The rules set forth here are a much simplified version of those presented by Dr. W. Edwards Deming.[1]

The following parameters are given:

P = fraction of incoming goods that are defective.

K_1 = cost to inspect (or test) one item.

K_2 = cost to later remove and replace the item if found defective after assembly into the product.

The rules of thumb are as follows:

If $P < \dfrac{K_1}{K_2}$, perform no incoming inspection.

If $P > \dfrac{K_1}{K_2}$, perform 100 percent incoming inspection.

The rule is simple enough, but it assumes that a choice is being made based on economics only. We know, however, that there are other considerations besides those expressed by this pair of formulas.

100 Percent Inspection

Inspecting every item is called *100 percent inspection* or *screening*. This process should result in rejection of all nonconforming items and acceptance of all good items; but it is not that simple. An alternative, sampling plans, were developed for several reasons:

1. The process of 100 percent inspection is expensive and time-consuming.
2. Such inspections are inadequate due to human error, monotony, and overlooking defects.

1. W. Edwards Deming, *Quality, Productivity, and Competitive Position* (Cambridge, Mass.: MIT Press, 1982).

3. Supplier's lack the incentive to ship all good items if they know customers will sort them.
4. Some tests are destructive.

Recently, however, the use of automatic testing and inspection equipment has been able to eliminate the first two drawbacks. This means that when the supplier claims it uses 100 percent inspection, the buyer needs to ascertain just what is being checked and how it is being done, by machine or humans.

Acceptance Sampling

An acceptance sampling plan is applied to a lot (or batch) of items to determine if the items in the lot meet the standards. In acceptance sampling, a sample of predetermined size, n, is to be taken from a lot if size N. If the number of defectives exceeds the acceptance numbers, c, the lot is rejected. Otherwise, the lot is accepted. If we were inspecting a unit, we could count defects per unit rather than number of defectives.

We will deal here only with single sampling (the simplest form), where one sample is taken from each lot and a decision to accept or reject is based on the one sample. Consider an example:

$$N = 500$$
$$n = 50$$
$$c = 3$$

We select a random sample of fifty items from the lot of five hundred. If three or fewer are defective, we accept the lot. If four or more defectives are found, we reject the lot.

Advantages of Acceptance Sampling

There are a number of reasons for using acceptance sampling rather than 100 percent inspection as follows:

1. Sampling is more economical, as it requires fewer inspections and thus fewer inspectors.

2. Less product handling takes place, and therefore, damage is less likely.
3. Inspection is less monotonous, and with fewer items to be inspected, the likelihood of error is reduced.
4. Some inspections or tests are destructive, and in such cases, sampling *must* be used.
5. A sampling plan provides a predetermined sample size and acceptance number, based on statistical concepts, and the numbers are not left to inspector judgment.
6. Plans provide for rejection of entire lots if c, the acceptance number, is exceeded. This system better motivates the producer to submit good quality and take corrective action on rejects.

Disadvantages of Acceptance Sampling
Sampling plans also have disadvantages as follows:

1. There are risks of accepting bad lots and rejecting good lots.
2. Time and expertise are needed to set up valid sampling plans and negotiate them with suppliers.
3. Information available is limited to data from the sample.
4. When entire lots are rejected, production personnel may try to force quality control personnel to sort a shipment to keep production going.
5. Everyone involved must be constantly reminded that acceptance sampling is done under the premise that the process mean value is known. In addition, a specific sampling plan, such as one that specifies 1.5 percent AQL, will most often accept material that actually has 1.5 percent defects. On a lot-by-lot basis, then, the actual lot quality could be significantly worse than the AQL level. This occurs particularly with relatively small sample sizes.

Establishing Lots

The effectiveness and efficiency of sampling is influenced by the way the lots are formed. The following are some rules to establish lots for sample purposes.

1. Lots should be homogeneous. For example, all items in a lot should be produced in the same batch, by the same machine, and the same operator.
2. It is most efficient to use lots as large as possible.
3. Lots should be suited to shipping containers, vehicles, and materials handling equipment. For example, a keg or a truckload would be designated as a lot.
4. The selection of the sample should be easily accomplished. Avoid selecting the sample by sorting and counting.

Advance vs. On-Arrival Sampling

Sometimes a purchaser arranges to inspect a sample of goods before receiving the shipment. The supplier, for example, may ship a selected sample of the material to the buyer. Upon receipt, the buyer inspects or tests it and notifies the supplier if the results are not acceptable. There are several disadvantages to this type of arrangement.

1. The sample items received may not be representative of the entire lot.
2. Damage or contamination may have occurred during shipment.
3. Unethical practices may have occurred, such as *salting*— that is, adding known defectives to a good lot while maintaining the percentage of defectives below the limits specified by the purchaser.

Stationing a buyer's representative at the supplier's facility can alleviate the first and third problems.

On-arrival inspection or testing also has some disadvantages. First and foremost, inspection at the source can better eliminate or reduce the receipt of defective lots than can on-arrival inspection. Furthermore, inspection time, delays in start of testing, and holding until acceptance decisions are made are costs to the buying company. There are also the problems related to holding rejected lots for disposition and associated production problems related to rejected shipments.

Special Considerations in Inspection and Testing

The following are some special situations that should be dealt with separately in planning for inspection and testing.

Software

The term *software* refers to any computer program, and a program can be priced and delivered as part of the associated hardware or separately. It may be loaded as part of the manufacturing process and unalterable, or loadable by the user.

In controlling quality of any product, we can speak of the *quality of design* (i.e., does the product meet the needs of the user?) and the *quality of conformance* (i.e., does a particular item conform to the design requirement?). Software quality can be evaluated in the same way.

Testing software for acceptance essentially involves checking the outputs that the software system generates. The number of possible outputs for the system can be very large, however, and it is hardly possible to check all of them. This produces a situation in which statistical sampling procedures could apply. If a sample of outputs, m, is checked and n outputs are found to be acceptable, then the rate of defectives is $\frac{m-n}{m}$. Generally, it is best to take a random sample of the outputs.

As in any supplier quality strategy, it is preferable for the test to be performed at the supplier's facility, subject to verification by the purchaser. The test could be witnessed at the supplier's facility, or could be furnished with the delivered software. Careful planning is required if the software is to be tested upon receipt by the buyer.

Quality of Services

Measuring quality of services is usually more difficult than measuring product quality, but it is just as necessary. Important factors in a service are timeliness, accuracy, and completeness of the service performed. Examples of services are security, housekeeping, delivery, or cafeteria service. As with a product, the first step in quality planning is for the customer to define what he or she wants—that is, the requirements. Next, possible discrepancies are identified as well as their importance.

Since services are usually labor intensive, attempts to improve productivity will often occur at the expense of quality. Just as with products, however, if rework is charged against productivity, no matter how much later the service discrepancy is found, we see that improving quality also enhances productivity.

The feedback from complaints is an important element in measuring quality of service. The buyer of services should store the data in a manner that allows problems to be easily identified as the data accumulates so that corrective action can be initiated.

Automatic Testing Equipment

Automatic testing and inspection equipment has removed many of the major disadvantages previously associated with 100 percent inspection or testing. The automatic equipment allows more consistent checking, results in fewer errors, and can be operated at lower per-unit testing cost. Besides the lower cost due to increased speed of checking, the equipment can be operated by less skilled operators.

There are, however, disadvantages related to the use of automatic test equipment. The cost of the equipment is greater—though, for high-volume use, the equipment often pays for itself. Also, since automatic test equipment is more complex, failures can result in downtime or costly maintenance.

Computer-Aided Inspection and Testing

Considerable progress has occurred recently in the application of computers, along with advanced sensor technology, to automate inspection. Usually the computer-aided inspection is performed on 100 percent of the items and is preferably on-line as part of the production process. In the literature, we encounter the terms *computer-aided quality control* (CAQC), *computer-aided test* (CAT), and *computer-aided inspection* (CAI). This approach provides opportunities to use inspection results to make compensating adjustments in the manufacturing operation. It results not only in improved product quality but also in improved productivity.

The actual automated inspection can be performed with robots equipped with mechanical probes or sensing devices. The use of noncontact sensors is becoming more prevalent, since it reduces the part repositioning required for a contact-inspection device. The noncontact sensing devices include optical techniques, electrical inductance or other field measurement, radiation techniques, or ultrasonic methods. The noncontact inspection methods are usually much faster than the contact methods and eliminate potential damage to the part being inspected.

There are different degrees of computer-aided testing. In the more advanced applications, the product is automatically positioned and attached to the testing apparatus. The computer then monitors, analyzes, and sometimes, records the results. If the product passes the test, it is automatically moved to the next operation. If it fails the test, it is set aside for further diagnosis and disposition, usually performed manually.

Reliability Tests

The measurement of reliability is based on how well a supplier's product performs in service after having demonstrated initial acceptable performance. If it fails in service, the product's reliability may be deficient. Reliability failures create problems and considerable concern, since they often affect public safety. These defects are the most difficult to trace to an assignable cause, since information on the product may not be available or may be difficult to trace. Special reliability tests can be performed as part of qualification tests used to qualify a product design, or by taking sample items from lots for testing. These tests are designed to catch potential failure before the product goes to the customer. For the reliability data to be meaningful, samples that are representative of the lot must be taken. At times, particular parts are selected for testing rather than being selected at random. The results of such testing would give no correlation to the actual parts built.

Recording Testing and Inspection Data

Results of tests and inspections are the bases for acceptance or rejection of goods. Therefore, the recording of data on the results is important. It serves as backup in case questions arise about the decision and can also help solve problems that arise later. The logging and maintenance of inspection and test data are especially important with respect to supplier's items. For example, the data can substantiate a rejection that is questioned by the supplier. If the goods are accepted, the data becomes very useful in resolution of problems arising subsequent to the incoming inspection.

In cases where the inspection is performed by the supplier before shipping the goods, data furnished with the shipment can facilitate verification upon receipt. In some cases, the receiver can spot-check by testing specific items and comparing measurements to those furnished by the supplier. The identification of any discrepancies in measurement between purchaser and supplier is helpful in preventing further problems. Sometimes corrections in equipment calibration can be made at this time.

Test data can be either automatically or manually recorded. Automatic testing equipment often has strip printers or graphic recording devices. In many cases, it is desirable to place a copy of the test results with the product being tested as well as to retain a copy in the file. All data should be dated, written in ink, and signed by the person performing the test or inspection. Any corrected records should not obliterate erroneous data. All these reports are important for future quality audits or for resolving problems with the supplier that arise later.

Creating standardized forms for recording data is also important. This helps to ensure that all required checks are made. It also facilitates later verification of data. For elaborate tests, or acceptance of certain lots of material, it may be necessary to prepare a formal report of the results, possibly including conclusions and/or recommendations. This is especially important to qualification testing.

Inspection records should include the following:

- Part number
- Supplier (more than one may be used)
- Supplier's identifying number
- Measurements taken
- Tools or instruments used
- Sampling plan, if used
- Results
- Whether or not a supplier has been fully qualified
- Drawing or specification revision status
- Notes describing special requirements or measurements

It is unlikely that all characteristics will have the same sampling plan, so a separate space is needed for each characteristic measured. As noted earlier, testing and inspection data should be retained for future use if problems occur in production or after shipment.

During training, inspectors should learn to scan the inspection data for unusual items and changes in performance. For example, assume the sampling inspection requires a sample size of fifty (1.5 percent AQL, normal level II plan, with an accept on two defectives and reject on three defectives). A change would be represented if a lot were received with two defectives after the first five lots were received with no defectives. Even though this level meets the acceptance criteria, it indicates that the process has changed.

Problems and Corrective Action

Chapter 9

Every company needs a method to ensure that corrective action is taken to remedy problems or correct unsatisfactory conditions. Problems often involve nonconforming goods received from suppliers. We define *corrective action* as an activity that prevents further occurrence of an unsatisfactory condition. With respect to suppliers, corrective action would ensure that further shipments of goods do not contain the nonconformity. The effectiveness of the action depends on the degree of discipline involved in implementing it, and can be measured by success in achieving solutions.

Obtaining successful corrective action on supplier-provided goods is often more difficult than correcting internal problems. This is because factors such as poor communication, differing interpretations of contracts, language differences, and third-party involvement interfere with achievement of effective action. Procedures to achieve corrective action with suppliers must be designed to overcome these barriers.

The biggest problems with achieving corrective action are that (1) people are often afraid to admit there is a problem and (2) they tend to kill the messenger and not the problem. Thus, a fresh attitude is called for: (1) All problems are good, (2) a known problem is a solvable problem, and (3) a problem is a fact. Masking the problem will not change the facts. Getting upset at the facts will not change a bad problem. Finally, by using certain skills, all problems can be solved or abated.

What Is Corrective Action?

People often view corrective action as the fix needed to make the nonconforming item usable. This is a dangerous attitude that can delay or negate effective problem solving. Corrective action offers a permanent solution, not merely action to alleviate the pressure related to accepting a specific lot of material. If the corrective action is adequate, the particular nonconformity should not appear again. A critical part of any corrective-action system is feeding back information to the source of the problem, and follow-up to ensure that the problem—or similar problems—will not occur again.

Forms of Corrective Action

The following are examples of corrective actions that may result from analyses of problems:

1. Design or redesign of tools or fixtures
2. Further training of operator(s)
3. Exhibition of nonconforming items for all to see
4. Changes of process-control charts
5. Changes in engineering drawings or other design changes
6. Increased inspection until problem is resolved
7. Revision of material-handling methods
8. Changes in material identification
9. Segregation of nonconforming items

Examples

In each case below, assume you are the quality control engineer and have been given proposed corrective actions as a result of defectives found. Evaluate each. Would you accept the corrective action proposed? What additional questions should you ask?

a. A batch of fuel gages for motorcycles was rejected because about 10 percent showed one-quarter full when the tank was empty. Procurement notified the supplier, who provided instructions for adjusting the gages. This saved the cost of returning the lot.

b. An inspector measured three parts just machined and found all three above the upper tolerance. The operator checked the parts, agreed with the finding, and agreed to take corrective action by replacing a worn tool.

c. When the battery charger on a finished motorcycle did not operate correctly, the tester found the wrong size resistor in a circuit. In checking further, he found several more in other units. The assembly department later reported that receiving inspectors had accepted them in spite of the fact that they were marked incorrectly. Incorrect labeling led to inadvertent use in the wrong application. Therefore, the assembly department said quality control should pay for the replacement.

The above actions do not fully constitute corrective action. In problem *a* we should ask the following questions:

• Why were the gages not adjusted properly by the supplier before shipment?

• What was the cost of performing the adjustments at the user plant, and who is to pay for it?

• What will the supplier do to prevent further shipment of improperly adjusted gages?

In problem *b* we should ask the following:

- Why didn't the operator know the tool was worn before the inspector noticed it?
- Is there a problem with this tool only, or does the operator check any tools for wear?
- Does the operator have the equipment to check the work?
- Is the operator aware that it is his or her responsibility to ensure quality, and not the inspector's?

Problem *c* illustrates several user problems, but essentially, the supplier needs to be brought into the problem and to pay for the rework caused. The attitude of the assembly department is also of concern—punitive action against quality control will not solve the problem.

Evaluation of Defect

Many companies don't provide the supplier a firsthand opportunity to evaluate the defect. In some cases, analysis of the defect or failure is performed without the supplier's participation and perhaps without providing an opportunity to review the discrepancy. This is not only unfair to the supplier, but it may also delay the accomplishment of corrective action. On the other hand, prompt action is often advisable, since the supplier may not have the expertise or equipment to perform an adequate evaluation. This occurs when complex analyses of the overall product are required to determine the basic cause of a problem. In other cases, time is of the essence in identifying the problem without disrupting production schedules.

However, regardless of the approach, the supplier should be given the opportunity to evaluate nonconforming goods firsthand and should be provided with all pertinent information on a timely basis.

Notifying a supplier of a defect in material many months after it is used causes difficulties for that supplier. Sometimes simple changes in a supplier's personnel or production setups can locate causes of problems. Perhaps a new die designed to meet higher production rates was not used during a low-production period, and the substitution resulted in a problem. Timeliness can easily be designed into a corrective action system. The following are some roadblocks to timeliness that should be avoided:

1. Requirement of multiple signing of defect forms before a request for corrective action is made to supplier
2. Requirement that all communications be transmitted through a particular outside agency
3. Requirement of complete defect analysis prior to supplier notification

Case Example. One company had a corrective action system requiring that several departments as well as customers sign the defect form. It also required the customer to transmit the request for corrective action to the vendor. In one case, the vendor received first notification of the defect eighty-five days after it was found and after several thousand parts with similar defects were produced. This resulted in lost production by both supplier and user. Could the corrective action system of your company cause a situation like this?

At times, isolating the root cause of a problem may be impossible. The facts that caused it may have been transitory, or they may not be available during the investigation. For example, the specific lot of raw material might have been consumed before the defect is identified. In these cases, methods for isolating similar defects early in the process must be installed. If the problem recurs, a countermeasure could be developed.

Supplier Notification

As was just pointed out, communicating with the supplier about nonconforming goods is a first step in obtaining corrective action. Yet
operations often omit this step. The ailment can take many forms: no
formal method may exist for handling defects, parts are not actually
returned to the supplier, failures found during assembly are not
reported to the functions that should seek corrective action, suppliers
are not charged for defectives, or no action is taken by purchasing to
follow up and correct the nonconformity. Each one of these is an
essential step in obtaining effective correction. Company executives
often hear a supplier say, "I never heard about the condition," even
though the problem has existed for several months. This is not an
uncommon occurrence.

Other conditions can also develop: The rejection rate of incoming lots rises to 15 percent, assembly line stoppages occur weekly as
a result of defective supplier parts that are passed through to inventory stock, scrap and rework costs for supplier-caused defects exceed
reasonable levels, and sales are lost due to customer's complaints
about poor material or poor product performance.

These could be described as supplier problems, but they really
are the result of poor communication. Most suppliers want to perform
well. The user must take the first step by communicating effectively
with suppliers.

Good communication with suppliers is a key element of achieving corrective action. The method of communication can vary, but
should achieve maximum effectiveness. Telephone calls, letters,
returned material, visits, and charges back to suppliers should all be
used promptly to achieve the desired results. The supplier can be considered an extension of in-plant communications and part of a coordi-
nated effort to achieve corrective action. This approach helps to
reduce the number of defective lots received and obtain quicker resolution of discrepancies that do occur.

Buyer-Supplier Interaction

In all communications with the supplier, the buyer should set the tone and establish priorities. The buyer is the individual responsible for selecting a supplier and negotiating prices. Without buyer involvement, prompt corrective action may not occur, and confusion may result—especially when a supplier is being considered for further purchases. The buyer also provides the channel for monetary charges to the supplier.

Telephone Contact

The telephone is a fast and effective method of communication with the supplier about nonconforming goods and problems. Since the parts are not directly available to the supplier, however, a telephone discussion can lead to misunderstandings. Due to other pressures on the supplier, a phone call may fail to produce effective corrective action. A follow-up call is usually needed to confirm the need for corrective action or to ensure that action was taken. In all cases, the call should be made in a professional manner, and all information affecting the discrepancy should be available at that time. This will reduce confusion and make the call more effective.

If too many problems are occurring to allow calling all the suppliers involved, a few problem suppliers can usually be identified for initial action. Suppliers who are supplying parts with multiple defects are likely candidates. An effective quality system should incorporate a log of phone calls—containing the name of the individual called, date, main elements discussed, and date of promised action.

Written Notification

Although phone contact has its advantages, it doesn't provide a written response by the supplier. An effective and inexpensive system for notifying suppliers of defects can be developed through the use of a multiple-copy form. The form, consisting of four copies, provides (1) a permanent record of the defect and disposition of material, (2) a copy to transmit to the vendor for analysis and corrective action (copy 2), (3) a copy for the buyer's quality control organization (copy 3; this copy can also be used in a follow-up file to provide a reminder that a written supplier response is needed), and (4) a copy for return with the defective material to supplier if the material is being returned.

Timely transmittal of the form is important. A good system ensures that the request for corrective action is transmitted to the supplier within twenty-four hours of discovery of the defect. Timeliness of the transmittal can prevent the supplier from shipping further goods with the same problem, resulting in another rejection. Many suppliers will call back upon receipt of the malfunctioning goods, to obtain more details or seek information that will clarify a discrepancy.

As with the phone call, care must be taken in describing a defect so that as much information as possible is given. The description of the defect also must be accurate and clear. It is easy to fall into a trap of describing a defect as "the hole size is too large," or "the resistance is too high." Even if there were only one hole in the part, or one resistance measure, these are not adequate descriptions. The defect description should include the following as a minimum:

- The characteristic that is nonconforming
- The test or inspection equipment used to evaluate the part
- Significant environmental conditions present during the discovery of the defect
- The frequency with which the defect has occurred

The following description is more appropriate than "the hole is too large" and is more likely to result in corrective action by a supplier:

The 1.000 ± .002 located as shown on Sheet 2 grid A-1 of print 329Y634 measures oversized 1.0025 to 1.003. The hole was measured by using wedged plug gages. Twelve of

125 pieces measured exceed print requirements. Similar defects were found on 2 of the last 3 lots received.

Leaving out any portion of this information will tend to delay obtaining effective corrective action.

Internal Actions
Communicating with the supplier doesn't complete the total cycle. Internal actions at the user's facility may be required to re-educate inspectors, revise inspection planning to ensure finding the defect on future lots, or revise blueprints to provide clarification. Whatever is done, however, should be communicated to the supplier to ensure adequate supplier effort in resolving future problems.

Steps in Corrective Action

Corrective action involves two processes:

1. Solving particular problems
2. Identifying root causes of problems from available records of failures and discrepancies

The steps in a valid corrective action system might be defined as follows:

1. Problem recognition and identification
2. Gathering of information from appropriate sources
3. Evaluation of information
4. Generation of alternative solutions
5. Selection of a solution from alternatives
6. Follow-up to secure action
7. Securing awareness of the problem on the part of all concerned, including management

8. Recording and disseminating information and evaluating results of actions taken so that problems are resolved and do not recur

Visit by Purchaser to Supplier's Facility

Visiting the supplier as part of the discrepancy analysis and corrective-action implementation should not be overlooked. Visiting the supplier has many advantages but certain limitations also. Besides providing an opportunity for assessing or reassessing the supplier's quality and manufacturing system, the visit allows firsthand observation of the supplier's attitude and approach to quality, technical strengths, handling of defectives, and management commitment to resolution of quality problems.

To illustrate, take a case in which a common part discrepancy might be revealed by a mechanical measurement made using a surface plate. If the buyer finds the supplier's surface plate covered with dust, he or she sees the supplier's commitment to meeting print requirements and following the basics of an inspection system are questionable. One other advantage of visiting the supplier is the possibility of identifying additional problems, which if not caught in the early stages, would become more serious and result in subsequent rejections. During a visit, key management individuals can also be contacted to ensure proper priorities and to obtain a commitment to resolving discrepancies and performing the required corrective action.

Quality Audits

Witch hunts are not audits. If the intention of an audit is to show the supplier why poor quality is being produced, then the audit should not be conducted. Audits should be done for the purpose of helping the supplier. They can, however, cause bad feelings or poor direction even if the results are favorable. For example, in some cases, the supplier might think that improvement is not necessary.

Audits for quality can be of several types:

1. System audits—to determine the effectiveness of the overall quality system and the degree to which quality objectives are achieved
2. Product audits—to determine fitness for use of the product by the intended customer
3. Procedure audits—to ascertain whether established procedures are being followed by inspectors, testers, operators, material handlers, and so on.

The quality audit provides a further opportunity to see exactly how the supplier ensures quality. What measures are used, and how does the supplier know what the outgoing quality is? Where are the checks made, and how involved is each? Were the right people at the supplier's plant aware of the rejected material or complaints from customers? If not, are there provisions for communicating problems to the people who can really take the corrective action?

An audit provides the opportunity to see how rejections are actually handled by the supplier. It is also a chance to examine records of past discrepancies received from users to see what was actually done about them. What about cases where the user did not return nonconforming items to the supplier? Was any action taken by the supplier? In general, it is a chance to observe actions a supplier takes to establish disposition, corrective action, verification of the fix, and recurrence prevention—the final determination of whether corrective action is to be successful.

Figure 9.1 shows three aspects of a quality audit of a supplier—or of a self-audit a company may decide to perform.

Visit by Supplier to Purchaser's Facility
Inviting a supplier to come to the plant and review a discrepancy provides an opportunity to develop a meaningful relationship.

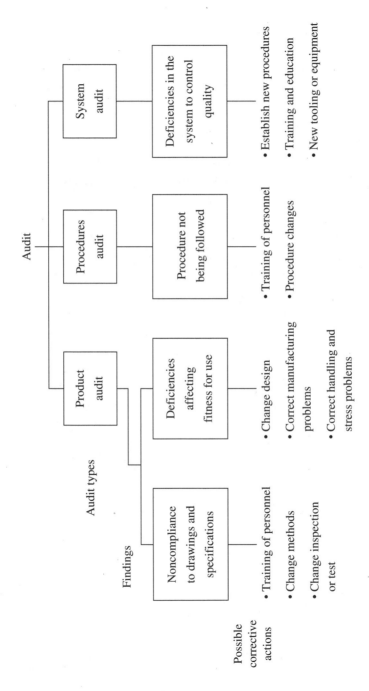

Figure 9.1   Quality audit.

During the visit, a review of where and how the supplier's product is used as well as the impact of part discrepancies can be discussed and displayed. Situations can be illustrated to the supplier: the difficulty of repairing items, the impact of defect on employee productivity and production schedules, and the effect on the customer if the final product is defective. The visit can give a supplier a better picture of his or her responsibility and the role of the supplier's materials in the finished product. The supplier could also assist in developing procedures for handling problems, discrepancy analysis, and design review. Finally, the visit enables the supplier to meet key individuals who are involved in the supplier's product design, production, and quality control.

Returning the Lot
Returning the rejected lot or material is an effective method of demonstrating the desire to obtain correction action. It provides the supplier firsthand information and an opportunity to analyze the defect. It also places the responsibility for sorting and/or rework at the origin of the discrepancy. Financial burdens are charged to the supplier in the form of transportation fees, lost productivity, and delayed billing. A clear description of the nonconformity should be included with the material, and the defective parts should be clearly segregated from the remainder of the lot. Any further information useful to the supplier in correcting or sorting the defects should also be included.

Charging a Supplier for Defects
All users' systems should have a means for requesting payment from suppliers when the users must do sorting, retesting, or rework caused by a supplier's nonconforming goods. These systems should be developed to include the purchasing operation and coordination through the buyer. The matter of whether the supplier will pay the full requested amount becomes negotiable. The supplier may refuse payment or may pay only a fraction of costs incurred. Even though no payment is received, a record of the cost incurred as a result of a

supplier nonconformity provides the information the buyer needs to negotiate new purchases.

If the requested charges are reasonable and reflect only the supplier's liability resulting from the discrepancies, there should be a good chance of collection from the supplier.

Consequential and Incidental Damages

We can define *consequential damages* as those resulting from nonconformity of an item, such as a user's repair costs, downtime, or injuries. These can often be substantial, amounting to more than the costs of the supplier items themselves. Suppliers are aware of this, so they frequently try to disclaim any responsibilities beyond the value of the item supplied. The UCC recognizes the user's right to consequential damages, but points out that the user has certain responsibilities in identifying and preventing use of nonconforming items.

The UCC is clearer in stating supplier responsibility for *incidental damages*, which are expenses reasonably incurred by the user in inspecting, receipt, handling, care, and custody of nonconforming goods. The user, however, must demonstrate that the method of computing these charges is reasonable. Further, a user is expected to implement reasonable inspection procedures upon receipt of goods. The cost of a buyer's efforts to get a purchased item to work properly can be deemed proper chargers to the supplier.

Material Review Board

Some facilities utilize the material review board (MRB) concept to assure adequate corrective action. The MRB would consist of an engineer and a quality control representative, at minimum. The board would meet periodically to review defective material, determine the cause, define the corrective action to be taken, and decide upon disposition of the defective material (such as repair, using it in the existing state, or scrap). Records of MRB actions are maintained, and recurrence of similar defects at a later time indicate inadequate corrective action.

Problem Suppliers

How can we determine which suppliers should appear on the list of problem suppliers? Problems holding up shipments, production lines, or use of equipment in the field almost automatically causes the responsible supplier to be placed on the list. A policy could be established by which a supplier's name is added, for example, whenever 4 percent of the supplier's lots have been rejected over the past three months. This criterion could be tightened or relaxed as needed.

The degree of seriousness of the defects causing the rejection should be considered also, since parts used "as is" create less trouble than those sent back, repaired, or scrapped. In some cases, the solution may be as simple as changing a part number; in other cases, a process or design at the supplier's plant may need to be changed. Sometimes the contractor may need to send technical assistance to help at the supplier's plant. This assistance would not, however, remove the responsibility for solving problems from the supplier.

Recurrence of Defects

Sometimes a company's quality objectives may allow a certain percentage of defects on the premises that zero defects is not economically practical. In that case, it becomes necessary to determine when recurrences of a defect exceed the allowable percentage. This makes it necessary to record defects, evaluate the quality data, and identify significant problems. When the recurrence of a defect is considered significant, corrective action is needed. A machine that is not set properly may produce 5 percent defects instead of 0.5 percent, as allowed. It may not be easy to notice this excessive level, however, without recording and evaluating data.

Attacking the Quality Problems

At some point, a company may recognize that quality problems exist with suppliers. However, a project may be too far along for management to implement all the techniques that constitute a good quality control program. For example, contracts may already exist without adequate standards. Or we may have a good program that still has quality problems. How do we start doing something to improve the situation?

First, purchasing must take the lead. The purchasing manager must make his or her personnel aware of their responsibilities. One way to start is to identify the biggest problems. They might be the most pressing problems, or the suppliers with an accumulation of lesser problems, or a combination of both. Most important, however, identifying the biggest problems gives us something to start working on. Second, the purchasing agent can contact each problem supplier and let the supplier know of his or her status as a problem supplier. The purchasing agent may worry that supplier X is the only available supplier, or the supplier may be offended and drop the buying company because, from the supplier's point of view, the company is only a small customer. That attitude, however, is not acceptable, and when pressure is applied, alternate sources can usually be found.

The problem suppliers should be brought into the plant. It is usually most effective to have a supplier's management people come in and see the problems that their defectives are causing. This works better than sending contractor's personnel to see and hear the supplier's pitch on how good they are and how nice their plant looks. In other words, when the supplier comes in, the buyer controls the topics of discussion and who participates. The buyer should point out that the supplier has a problem that must be solved to meet the contract requirements and that it is the supplier's responsibility to solve it. Acceptance of responsibility by the supplier goes a long way toward successfully resolving the problem.

Weaknesses and Strengths of a Corrective Action System

We have said that successful corrective action means permanent correction of a problem. There are, however, several weaknesses in corrective action systems that are important to identify:

1. Emphasis on quick fixes to make the product usable
2. Excessive delays in communicating information on failures to those responsible
3. Jumping at conclusions as to causes of nonconformities
4. Failure to bring problems to the attention of top management
5. Neglect of deficiencies that come to the supplier's attention after shipment
6. Failure to price nonconformances and attempt to recover the cost from supplier
7. Failure to consider past nonconformances and corrective actions in new source selection

An effective corrective action system will contain the following elements:

1. Discrepancies are well-defined and reported quickly.
2. Each problem is validated to establish its importance with respect to effect on quality of the final product, costs, and impact on schedules.
3. A diagnosis is made of causes of the nonconformity and the corrective action needed to permanently resolve the problem.
4. Assignment of responsibility for corrective action is made, and a schedule established for completion.
5. Determination is made as to whether other suppliers' items have similar problems.
6. Follow-up is done to ascertain that the problem has been solved.
7. A procedure is implemented to collect costs of supplier's nonconformances from supplier.

Working Relationships with Suppliers

Chapter 10

A close and positive working relationship between customer and supplier is a big factor in receiving quality products or services from a supplier. Earlier chapters in this book have covered the more technical aspects of obtaining quality from suppliers at the right price and on the required schedule. These responsibilities of the purchasing department—in particular the buyer—are often quite demanding. The buyer must possess the skills to deal with a variety of people in many different situations. For example, the buyer must establish and maintain a professional working relationship between the purchasing company and the supplier. In addition, the buyer must maintain clear lines of communication and responsibility to the various groups within his or her own organization, such as engineering, quality control, and production.

Past Practices and Current Goals

In past years, many companies relied on incoming inspection to verify the quality of items and material received. This was usually done at the purchaser's facility, but could also be done at the supplier's plant prior to shipment. Over the years, the trend has been toward greater reliance on the supplier's quality system, and recently this trend has gained momentum. The ultimate goal, then, would be complete elimination of inspection upon receipt by the purchaser. The ability to do this successfully depends upon the purchaser establishing a very favorable working relationship with the supplier. In most cases, buyers are reluctant to completely eliminate inspection upon receipt of the products. As a result, limited checking continues. Many Japanese and U.S. plants, however, have created a relationship with specific suppliers whereby there is essentially no incoming inspection.

Responsibility for Quality

A workable supplier relationship places the responsibility for furnishing quality items on the supplier. Emphasis is placed on the supplier's use of a well-designed product and a quality program that result in quality items being produced. The purchaser then requires evidence that this program continues in effect and that the items do meet the quality requirements. The supplier can provide this evidence in the form of data showing results of tests and inspections it performed, backed by the buyer's knowledge of the supplier's ability to control quality in the products. The purchaser may specify requirements for the supplier's quality system but may also place inspection requirements in the contract.

Quality Is Firm

The requirements in the purchase order must be considered firm, not as variables. Implications by the buyer that something must only be "good enough" will send the wrong message. In other words, both the buyer and the purchase order must be specific and firm so that everyone involved is absolutely clear on what is required. If the buyer does not take this firm approach, the supplier can hardly be expected to meet the requirements. One way to clarify expectations is to return nonconforming material to the supplier and insist that only material meeting requirements be shipped.

Too often companies give the impression to their suppliers that compliance with requirements is not a serious business. Buyers, engineers, and quality personnel apologize for the rejection of defective material, or depend on waivers or material review actions in order to avoid returning the material. When this type of approach is commonplace within a company, the supplier naturally takes advantage of the complacency. Actually, the supplier is led by this complacency to believe that the requirements are not needed or are unimportant. If unimportant, a requirement should be deleted.

What is the payoff for establishing a firm attitude in dealings with the supplier? The primary objective of a quality program is to have good material sent the first time. When a firm attitude is established, a company is more likely to receive usable items on time so that production schedules can be met. This contributes to productivity as well as to the possibility of reducing or eliminating receiving inspection or testing. The Japanese have done this with the just-in-time inventory concept, where little or no receiving inspection is performed, and items arrive at the point of use in production as they are needed. If not right, the product is corrected immediately by supplier sorting or corrective action.

Cost of Quality

As stated by Harold A. Berry, "The cost of quality is never so high as when it is missing."[1] The buyer must be concerned with the total cost, and not just the price that will appear on the invoice for the orders. The total cost includes costs related to poor quality—such as costs of rejections, return of shipment, repairs, production delays, and costs

1. Harold A. Berry, *Purchasing Guide* (Englewood Cliffs, N.J.: Prentice Hall, 1964), chap. 6.

related to customer receipt of products not fit for use. The buyer, however, must be cautious not to pay more for goods if they are not actually of better quality, and this is often difficult to determine.

Supplier Quality Audits

Audits for quality were discussed in Chapters 4 and 9. A company should audit its suppliers on a periodic basis over the life of the contract. An audit is conducted in much the same way as the original survey, except that the purchaser checks for continuing compliance by the supplier. The form used during the survey could also be utilized in the audit (see Chapter 4 for survey form).

Continuing Cooperation

After the contract with a supplier is signed and in effect, there is a continuing need for good working relations between the contractor and supplier. This need applies through the stages of procurement, as shown in Figure 10.1. Each party must have certain information from the other that is essential to carrying out the contract. Whenever information is exchanged affecting the contractual agreement, the new information should be made part of the contract. This is especially necessary for changes or clarification of requirements that are to be verified upon receipt of the goods. The best approach is to not change design requirements except at specified times. This provides windows to ensure that excess obsolete materials are not produced. The only changes that should be made at other times are for delivery requirements to match production needs.

Information will also be exchanged that does not result in a contract change. This includes items such as acceptance or qualification test data from the supplier or discussions related to problems arising in either facility. Sometimes problems will result in the need for corrective action by one of the parties. The resolution of problems is important to each party, but it is not always easy to resolve them to both parties' satisfaction.

1. Define and specify the cost, delivery, and quality requirements for the particular application.

2. Select suppliers who are ready, willing, and able to meet
   requirements.

3. Ensure that there is a clear meeting of minds on the requirements. Ensure that supplier's management backs these
   requirements.

4. Verify that goods received meet requirements.

5. Make disposition of nonconforming material and ensure that
   corrective action is taken on the root cause of a problem.

Figure 10.1   Stages in procurement: value control.

Since the supplier's products are essential parts of the final product, any interruption to the supplier's delivery schedule affects the
overall production schedule. This is not tolerable. In a good supplier-
contractor working relationship, it is expected that the supplier will
advise the buyer well in advance of any expected or even possible
delivery delays. For example, the supplier should be expected to provide safety stock of material stored at its own facility to prevent such
situations. Moreover, the supplier should keep the contractor aware
of a pending labor strike and progress in negotiations. Knowledge of
quantities in inventory would also be helpful to the contractor in
scheduling partial shipments. Finally, favorable communications to
the suppliers are helpful when schedules are met or quality is in conformance. Communications are not only for problems or criticisms.

Relations between the buyer and supplier affect the flow of
communications and supplies between them, and service is reduced

when problems are encountered. Fast and effective service is often needed. Technical assistance before, during, and after the delivery is also important. It is necessary, however, to define the requirements for service and technical assistance as part of the agreement with the supplier.

Successful Supplier Programs

Many companies have developed their own quality programs, each unique in one way or another. Divisions within the same corporations often debate the merits of each approach. Still, certain features or characteristics tend to show up in the more successful programs.

1. Programs that are forced on a supplier are rarely successful.
2. Programs that tend to focus only on one part of an organization have been shown to be less successful. Successful programs require top management support and a sound product design.
3. For successful programs, quality is a consideration in all activities from strategy formulation to performance evaluation of managerial personnel; all persons in the company should view quality as part of their job. As decisions are made, the impact on product quality should be considered. Successful quality programs show evidence of open cooperation between persons in different parts of the organization.
4. The less successful programs tend to deal more with reaction than with action and more with placing the blame for problems than with preventing them.
5. Successful programs usually have quality professionals to design, implement, and measure results of the program.
6. Successful programs place emphasis on prevention of defects and on assistance to line operations.

7. Quality programs that measure the cost of poor quality and relate the costs to impact on earnings and profits tend to be more successful in achieving quality in their products. When a company places a dollar figure on quality (or lack of quality), it then finds it easier to invest funds in equipment, personnel, or research and development to attain that quality.

8. Finally, companies with successful quality programs measure quality in terms of customer satisfaction.

Quality Responsibilities

Many activities must be carried out to attain a quality product. Some of these are normally performed by people in the quality control organization; others rightfully belong in other parts of the organization. For example, manufacturing personnel have the responsibility to make products meeting the standards and specifications. It would not make sense for someone other than the person making or working on the product to check each step of the work as it was performed. Thus, the worker must have a means of determining that his or her own work has been done properly. This may involve a measurement, a means of controlling a process or machining operation, verifying software, or all of these.

Similarly, the engineer is responsible for producing a design that will meet the needs of the user and can be produced easily. It is up to the engineer to ascertain these needs by working with the customer's product definition and then working with the manufacturing engineer to assure that the design can be manufactured with the equipment available to the people in manufacturing. The engineer must also upgrade designs as advances are made in the customer's technology. If this does not occur, then improvements may be difficult.

What then are the responsibilities of the purchasing department? The purchasing agent is fully responsible for administering the contracts and purchase orders; she or he must make sure that the supplier provides parts, materials, or services that conform to the company's standards. The purchasing agent also has the responsibility to make sure that the supplier delivers material at the time scheduled. Defective parts are the same as no parts at all and can shut down production. Defective parts result in a significant amount of work for the buyer. The part must be returned and then reprocured and additional, expedited parts must be substituted. Besides schedule and quality constraints, the purchasing agent has the further responsibility to negotiate a price favorable to the contractor. It might be said that the purchasing agent has the job of selecting the supplier with the lowest price from among the potential suppliers who can meet the quality and schedule requirements. In performing these duties, the purchasing agent utilizes the services of engineers, production schedulers, and quality control engineers. Each of them has a special know-how or skill that can be helpful in purchasing items meeting all the requirements.

Purchasing and Engineering

The engineer determines what is needed in the product and part design to meet the needs of the user. If the design contains parts or materials to be procured from a supplier, the requirements these parts or materials must meet are given in the design drawings and specifications. Although the engineer may suggest possible suppliers for a particular part or material, it is the responsibility of purchasing to ensure that an appropriate supplier is selected. In some cases, the buyer may insist that the engineer evaluate alternative suppliers' products. In this selection process, the buyer may question requirements specified by the engineers if any appear unnecessary, but the final decision must always be based on the engineering drawings.

The prices quoted by suppliers depend upon the severity of the requirements to be met. In the interest of the company, price is important, but standards should not be sacrificed unless the engineer determines that the particular requirement can be relaxed. If the engineer finds that a requirement can be changed, the appropriate drawing or specification must be changed. The purchase order documentation, including the specification, must exactly describe the requirements, and the buyer or anyone else must obtain formal authorization of any changes. Specified requirements may be relaxed to reduce price, allow a standard item to be used, or permit the buyer to locate more bidders on the contract—but only if the needs of the product user are still met. In this process, anything unclear or ambiguous must also be corrected by the engineer. In general, an engineer who does his or her job well must consider the economics of obtaining or manufacturing the item and the advantages of having multiple sources, along with the necessary performance of the product.

Purchasing and Production

The production department is responsible for determining the schedules for manufacturing. These schedules are provided to the purchasing department, where a procurement schedule is prepared. Purchasing needs an adequate lead time to evaluate and select suppliers for each part and material. This is especially true if some items have not been procured previously, necessitating qualification tests to ensure that the items can meet the specified requirements. With an adequate lead time, a purchasing agent can do a better job of negotiating prices. Short lead times often result in special production runs, extra shipping costs, or missed delivery schedules, and can also result in failure to meet sales commitments, or even in shipment of products without completion of tests.

The lack of needed parts or raw materials can shut down processes or production lines. In a job shop, the results are less disastrous, but are still costly both in production delays and stoppages. In any case, frequent problems of this nature add to production costs and may result in loss of reorders or in dissatisfied users of the product. The purchasing agent, then, is told by production what to buy, how much, and when it is needed. Even so, the purchasing agent also has the duty to question these factors, to be knowledgeable of the latest products available, and to set sufficient lead times on orders. Perhaps an alternative material or a less expensive, standard item will suffice, especially if it is available now and the specified part is not. It is a responsibility of purchasing to be aware of new materials or parts as they become available and to question the design engineer and production scheduler as to their possible usage.

Sometimes an alternate part or material may cost more than the one specified or used in the past, yet the higher cost may be offset by lower in-house machining costs, longer life, or greater reliability. Both production and purchasing get involved in determining economical ordering quantities, since a large order may be received in partial shipments. Moreover, there are storage costs, shipping costs, and inspection costs to consider in selecting the lot size for shipment. One alternative is to order material on a firm, one-month-order basis but arrange for receipt of the material every other day, or as necessary to match production without the necessity of moving the material into inventory. Some companies define *on time* as −3 +1 days (i.e., if received up to three days prior or up to one day after the scheduled day, it is considered to be on time). Some companies use a 24-hour period to define an acceptable delivery window.

Clearly, purchasing becomes involved in trade-offs of important but sometimes conflicting company objectives. With good department interrelationships, however, these conflicts can usually be resolved in the day-to-day operations.

Purchasing as a Management Function

Within the company, purchasing is a part of the functional organization just like marketing, finance, manufacturing, personnel, and other functions. In this sense, purchasing is a member of the management team, which works together to attain a profitable enterprise with a good company image for quality, price, and delivery.

Quality System
Sometimes the term *quality system* is used to signify the collective group of activities, plans, and events that together are intended to ensure that a product, material, process, or service will meet the standards and

satisfy the user's needs. If customer satisfaction is not achieved, the system is not adequate. Clearly, the needs of a contractor or company purchasing items must be satisfied. In addition, the needs of the ultimate user of the product must be satisfied. Since the supplier is not always fully aware of the manner in which the product will eventually be used, the contractor must carefully define the requirements and standards the supplier's product must meet.

Companies use training and certification of employees to achieve compliance to requirements and standards, but motivation and attention to details are also needed. As an example, those with driver's licenses received training and were certified by the state issuing the license. Compliance, in contrast, involves following the speed limits. Does compliance, then, automatically follow from training and certification? Simple observation tells us that the answer is no. The supplier's objective will only be met, then, if the standards are correctly established, management provides the proper quality emphasis, and the quality control program provides the system for ensuring compliance.

The activities making up the system or program must be geared more to the avoidance of quality problems than to the resolution of problems after they occur. The system must be oriented toward making products correctly in the first place rather than recognizing and sorting the good items from the bad. The purchasing agent has the responsibility of integrating the company's activities with those of the supplier to ensure that the commodities meet all specified standards when they arrive on the receiving dock. Even if the defective items could be returned to the supplier for replacement at no cost, this course of action would not be satisfactory since the schedule may be adversely affected.

Products meeting the quality and reliability standards do not just happen. Achieving good quality through a successful quality system requires a commitment and investment by management. Management must provide the resources—especially people—to attain a successful system and keep it working without letup. A top-notch quality system does not permit relaxation; it provides the basis of an innovative and continuous process.

Information Flow

Responsibility for supplier quality has been assigned to the purchasing agent in previous chapters of this book. Having this responsibility, the agent must be aware of all communications with the supplier. For example, an engineer should not advise a supplier that a product deviation is acceptable without securing a change in the purchase order requirements or processing a formal approval. In the absence of proper authorization, receiving inspection should reject the deviating lot upon receipt. Such problems can be prevented, however, if the responsible purchasing agent is aware of all communications. Therefore, in most companies, all formal communications with the supplier go through the purchasing agent.

We do not mean to say, however, that no one besides the purchasing agent should talk to the supplier. For example, a resident engineer may be maintained at the supplier's plant. In that case, both companies should understand that discussions may result in tentative agreements, which must be followed up by the purchasing agent's ratification.

In conclusion, the best policy is for all information from suppliers to come into the company through the purchasing department. Likewise, all information going to the supplier should be sent by the purchasing department. This ensures that the buyers are aware of all communications and that conflicting information is clarified before being transmitted.

Figure 10.2 shows most of the information that may be transmitted back and forth on a contract and back and forth from buyer to other internal departments, though all of it does not apply to each subcontract. Some of the data is applicable to all contracts, while other information is needed only if specified in the purchase order as a requirement. In short, the only thing going to a supplier and bypassing the buyer should be the checks to pay a supplier. Perhaps even these checks should go through the buyer so she or he could have a chance to hold up payment or respond to the supplier's inquiries about payment.

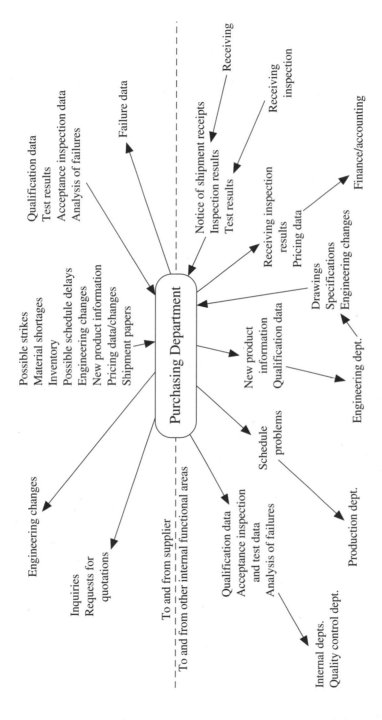

Figure 10.2 Flow of procurement information (current supplier).

Some Widely Used Concepts

For those dealing with suppliers and with other departments, an understanding of certain concepts is important. A few of these are described here and in other parts of this book.

Configuration Control

The term *configuration control* includes the control of design changes. In some cases, such as with newly developed products, it is not unusual to have many design changes. Since these changes can affect the form, fit, and function of the items with respect to the final product, a method must be established to provide close control. It is easy to imagine the problems that might occur if goods received from suppliers did not contain the design changes necessary to be compatible with the final product. The lack of a good drawing-change control system frequently causes friction between a contractor and the suppliers.

Corrective Action

It is essential to communicate with the supplier regarding any nonconformances found. A nonconformance may be found at receiving inspection, in the contractor's plant, or after shipment to the customer. Clarity and promptness are extremely important so that the supplier fully understands the problem as soon as possible. This may help prevent further manufacture of rejectable items by the supplier or further shipment of items with similar nonconformances. Often, the supplier can benefit from coming to the site where the nonconformance was identified or is occurring. This will not only give the supplier a more precise view of the situation, but will also permit the supplier to see the extent of the problem it has caused. (Corrective action was dealt with at greater length in Chapter 9.)

> **Case Example.** A receiving inspection organization was experiencing a 30 percent lot-rejection rate. Analysis showed that more than 80 percent of the lots were repeatedly rejected for the same reasons. Feedback to the supplier at the time

required two weeks. Evaluation showed that the repeat rejections occurred on material that was in transit during this two-week delay. When the receiving inspection department took the responsibility to notify the supplier within twenty-four hours of the rejection and also requested response within twenty-four hours, the rejection rate dropped by 15 percent. The majority of suppliers responded that engineering or purchasing had allowed the deviation by its previous delays. This brought out a serious management deficiency and communication problem in the purchasing company.

Traceability

Take a case where a product failure encountered during testing turns out to be the result of a supplied part. To solve the problems and improve quality, the purchaser must first trace the items to the supplier. If more than one company supplied the part, tracing is a mandatory first step—however, it is not usually sufficient. The buyer must also determine exactly when and where the quality problem originated. This means identifying the relevant tools, people, dates, work shift, or material at the facility where the items were made. If tracing is possible, we may be well on our way to preventing further occurrences. If we are unable to determine what went wrong and who was involved, corrective action becomes more difficult.

A system that provides traceability also has benefits in the prevention of defects. Our understanding of human behavior tells us that if a worker or inspector knows that defective work or defects overlooked in inspection can be traced back to him or her, errors might be avoided in the first place. Fear or pride in workmanship come into play when someone measures the quality and quantity of work done; traceability, therefore, increases the incentive for quality. If management is not able to trace a product, it can result in expensive recalls. One car company, in 1991, was required to recall fifty thousand cars due to suppliers' defects that were not traceable, whereas two other automakers only recalled the exact number of cars (fifty-six and thirty-six) that were known to contain defective items.

Some Japanese Ideas

Japanese manufacturers employ a variety of techniques and concepts different from those most widely used in the United States. Some of these will be summarized with regard to their impact on quality.

The Vital Few

The Japanese took the lead in employing complex problem-solving techniques to identify the vital conditions, or vital few, having the greatest impact on a product. This process included analysis of available data to find the root causes and make design or system changes that eliminate the root cause. This way, problems are eliminated permanently. Meanwhile, they also acted quickly to eliminate more obvious problems.

Order Quantities

Textbooks deal with the EOQ (economic order quality) concept, in which order costs are traded off against carrying costs to arrive at the optimal purchase-order size. The buyer may take advantage of blanket ordering and other techniques when selecting the order size. If sampling inspection is used to accept lots, its cost is included as part of the order costs along with shipping costs. Smaller order quantities tend to place a greater burden on incoming inspection, since sampling inspection requires that proportionately greater samples be inspected as the lot size decreases.

Consensus Decision Making

The Japanese system provides for involvement by many in the decision-making process. The primary strength of this approach lies in involvement of those responsible for the implementation of decisions reached. By this method, everyone is committed to making the decision work. If the decision were unilateral and made by only one department, the other departments would have less incentive to comply with the decisions. The system has certain drawbacks, however, including longer lead times necessary for reaching decisions and problems related to rapid technological change. In U.S. companies, supplier-related decisions usually involve representatives of several company functions—so we do utilize consensus decision making to some extent.

Just-in-Time (JIT) Purchasing

The JIT concept as utilized by the Japanese involves ordering so that quantities arrive as required to meet manufacturing needs. Often the orders are delivered directly to the production line stations without incoming inspection. This eliminates inventory warehousing and associated storage losses but places greater reliance on the supplier's quality control system. In some cases, the purchase order will specify an overall quantity to be released in segments as part of a longer-term production schedule. In some cases, manufacturing work centers are given order cards to release to the supplier as more items are needed.

Exact Shipment Size

In the United States, it is common practice for suppliers to ship more or less than the quantity specified for a shipment. Because of this policy, it is necessary to count items upon receipt in order to verify the quantity for payment. Most Japanese companies specify and accept only the exact quantity. Items are usually packaged in boxes with compartments so that it is easy to verify the quantity. Parts are usually well packaged with no overages to allow for damaged parts or defective items. An exact quantity of all good items is expected by the buyer, and usually, that is what is delivered. This method is the simplest from a production-control standpoint. Ordering and scheduling based on need are important as they result in the lowest cost.

On-the-Job Training

A Japanese employee receives in-company training until retirement as a regular part of the job. The employee is trained in skills related not only to his or her own job but to other jobs at the same level. Employees who have technical background, for example, are given responsibility in all the technical disciplines including design, quality engineering, and production engineering. Thus, they learn aspects of the business and its products and gain greater experience and commitment. This practice also provides considerable flexibility in the work force and helps develop people into generalists with a broader view of the company as a whole. In addition, it gives a person wider contacts within the company. For example, a purchasing agent with job experience in quality control might better perform the purchasing function. Likewise, a quality control engineer with purchasing experience would better perform the quality function. The best way to consider this is to imagine a case where a set of parts and set of engineering drawings are given to a U.S. firm and a Japanese firm. In the U.S. firm, higher variability and poorer product performance result. In the Japanese company, the product works with higher relative quality. The worker understands what is needed and improves the product.

Specifying Requirements

In the United States, design engineers tend to specify all requirements, including dimensions. The suppliers then must comply, or secure changes in requirements. The Japanese tend to simplify the specifications by relying more on performance requirements. This allows the supplier greater leeway for innovation in deciding how to meet the requirements. Critical dimensions would be given, allowing the supplier flexibility as long as performance requirements are achieved. This approach also reduces assembly requirements and relies on cooperation and good communication to achieve the desired performance.

Lifetime Employment

The Japanese policy of lifetime employment has less direct applicability to a purchasing-quality control program but tends to provide increased loyalty to a company. At the same time, however, it gives the company less flexibility to handle changing product demands, changes in technology, and down-turns in the economy.

Remuneration Based on Seniority

The Japanese system depends largely on a seniority-based wage plan, where the pay is determined primarily by the number of years worked. Wage differentials depend almost entirely on age and length of service.

This system eliminates the sometimes-destructive competition between individuals and promotes a more harmonious working relationship. It also assumes that a person's responsibilities will increase as seniority increases, which becomes more difficult in periods of slow growth or business recession. It also can be demoralizing to younger people, when opportunities for promotion are not available.

When Problems Occur

A typical scenario is set in motion when a quality problem occurs at a purchaser's facility. The supplier's component is assembled into the final product, but one-third of the finished units do not operate correctly. Negotiations with the supplier fail to correct the problem.

When Rejection Occurs

Once it is determined that a supplier's material does not comply with the requirements, prompt action is important. As noted earlier, the supplier must be informed immediately to prevent further production of defective items and to secure corrective action. Moreover, the defective materials must be replaced with good items as soon as possible. The buyer's production and manufacturing people also need immediate warning, since there is likely to be an impact on their production scheduling. The design engineer should be informed also, since she or he must determine the effect on performance of any products having the deficiency.

A supplier may react in different ways—but for now, let's assume that the supplier agrees that the item does not meet the requirement. Some possible supplier reactions, among others, are: (1) the items were satisfactory when shipped, (2) there was difficulty controlling the process, (3) the shipment is within the AQL, and (4) if the purchaser supplies appropriate data on the defects and defect samples, an analysis can be made and action taken.

When a supplier has continuing quality problems, one of the better approaches is to bring one or more of the supplier's people into the plant. Seeing a shutdown assembly line, piles of rejects, or other evidence often helps convince the supplier of the importance of the problem. Furthermore, the supplier should be expected to provide conforming parts in order to prevent further rejections and production shifts. It is best if the corrective action can be established while the supplier's people are present, or soon thereafter. The scheduling of the corrective action should allow the buyer to follow up and ensure that it is carried out. Elimination of the problem would, of course, be the final evidence of successful action. The corrective action should occur in two parts—short-term solutions and long-term actions involving correction of the root cause.

Some people might think that it is better to send a task force to the supplier's plant. This, however, places the travel-cost burden on the purchaser. It also allows the supplier to control the meeting and show off more attributes than problems. It further tends to shift some responsibility for identifying the source of the problem to the purchaser. Probably most important, however, is that the supplier does not witness the actual defective items as they impact on the purchasing company. If the supplier really lacks technical know-how, however, a visit to the supplier's plant may be the better solution. A visit to the supplier has the advantage of showing interest in the problem and the action taken to eliminate it. It can be used also to ensure that the supplier's management is informed of the problem.

If there is a visit to the supplier, the buyer should certainly participate. The design engineer and quality control engineer are also essential participants. One thing the visitors should ask about is the supplier's corrective action process. They should take a defective part and ask the supplier's people to go through the steps they take, starting from the time the buyer advises them of a problem. Does the procedure ensure that the defect will not occur again? What if the supplier's corrective action procedure is inadequate? The buyer's team can make some suggestions or show how their own procedure works.

Review of Rejected Material

The MRB takes action when rejected material is urgently needed on the production floor and might be usable even though there is a nonconformity. It may be possible to repair the item and use it, or the defect may be such that performance is not affected. In any case, allowing use of the item after MRB approval is not always contingent on defining the corrective action necessary to assure that material with the defects will not be received from a supplier again. Moreover, the fact that an MRB-approved use of the part is not a guarantee that parts are useable. An MRB review may not be able to determine usability of product, as all the defects may not be identified. If the product gives a problem, it should be rejected from use regardless of the MRB action.

It is certainly not appropriate to place rejected items before the MRB if the items are not urgently needed. MRB action may give the supplier a message that defectives may be all right after all.

The membership of the MRB varies but would generally include the design engineer, quality control, and the manufacturing unit that will be using the item. It also makes sense to invite the buyer, even though he or she has no vote. Typically, rejection by any one member would mean the item is returned to the supplier.

Decisions for acceptance would include (1) use as is, (2) use after specified rework, (3) repair the part, or (4) combination of the above. *Rework* is defined as return to print conformance, whereas *repair* is defined as not returning to print but to useable condition. In any case, however, acceptance can only take place if corrective action—which precludes receipt of further defective items—is obtained from the supplier.

Ongoing Performance Evaluation

In our discussions, we see that purchasing contributes significantly to the company and product quality. Other areas in which purchasing has an impact are those of price and schedule. Although it may be more difficult to measure purchasing's achievement in quality, this does not negate the need for performance evaluation. A readily available measure is the number (or portion) of rejected shipments (or items) received. The compilation of rejects should include those found at incoming inspection, later in manufacturing, or even after the customer receives the end product. By counting defects as nondelivered items, quality is placed on an equal level with delivery.

Measure of Success

Supplier-rating systems should be simple, should measure the key aspects of compliance, and should be easily understood by the supplier. The rating should consider delivery, quality, and conformance to paperwork. Delivery can be measured in parts per million of the total delivered early or late, divided by the total required. Quality can be measured by parts per million total defects (discovered during receiving inspection and production), divided by parts delivered. Finally, conformance to paperwork can be measured by number of trouble reports issued for incorrect or missing paperwork. If these factors are added for a combined rating, the evaluator must take care that a problem in one area is not masked by a low rating in another area. A score of zero is perfect.

We have discussed supplier-rating systems to evaluate suppliers (see Chapter 4), but the real source of success for a supplier's quality program is the buyer. With a supplier-rating system, the buyers choose from among the suppliers rated as satisfactory. A buyer-rating system, however, gives the buyer incentives to go beyond simply selecting the highest-rated supplier. The buyer can improve his or her own performance by obtaining continuing quality improvement.

One way to rate buyers, for example, is to measure the cost of poor quality. This cost would include the expense of rejections, rework, servicing, inspection, and test of replaced goods, design changes related to defective work or delayed schedules due to lack of supplied items. The cost could be measured as a percentage of payments to the suppliers.

Alternatives and Trends

Chapter 11

A s we continue to move more and more into a global economy, old standards for measuring value and quality are falling by the wayside. Fast and low-cost transportation and communication methods are reducing the former strategic advantages of location and natural resources. Many manufactured items contain the labor and resources of several countries. This is true of many products sold in the United States. Companies are also seeing new competitors arise in surprising places around the globe. All of this means that buyers acquire greater ability to choose as power shifts from those who sell to those who buy. Quality, defined in new ways, has become the predominant standard with which suppliers can hold customer loyalty.

The Supplier's Challenge

To compete in today's—and the future's—marketplace, companies have recognized that they must furnish products that the consumer recognizes as desirable in quality and price. Any supplier faces this challenge, because the purchasing organization, as the immediate consumer, has increased the emphasis on these objectives. Thus, all members of both the supplier's and the buyer's organizations must comprehend the importance of quality and the tie between quality, improved productivity, reduced expenses, and increased sales. This recognition of the importance of quality is enhanced by a strong commitment from higher levels of management. This concept appears to be winning a stronger foothold in U.S. companies, prompted by competition from foreign sources.

The earlier chapters of this book deal with quality as part of subcontracting strategy, tactical planning and execution by purchasing to include definitions of quality, continuing assessment of quality, and follow-up where necessary to ensure that quality is achieved. Most of these concepts and techniques are not new—they have been tried and proven over many years. However, the integration of these concepts into a strategy—and its implementation—can provide a basis for a new look at the total quality-purchasing operation.

Quality Trends

Several U.S. products that were traditionally considered by the world to be superior have more recently been perceived as inferior. Examples are automobiles, electronic equipment, and textiles. Are we saying that the quality of U.S. products has declined? Actually, the quality of U.S. products is higher now than it has ever been. Compare the latest television, computer, or typewriter with an older model to establish this fact. What, then, has happened to foster this perception of diminished quality? Basically, some foreign companies have increased their share of the market by providing superior quality at equal or lower prices. We can conclude that the quality of U.S. products has not declined, but rather that some products manufactured in other countries have surged past ours in quality. Figure 11.1 illustrates this trend.

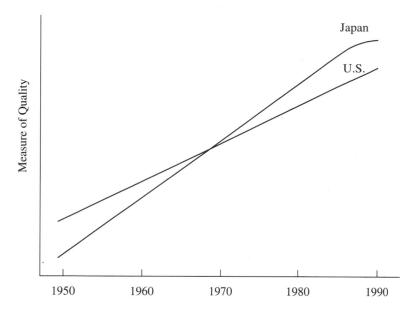

Figure 11.1   Comparative quality trends.

Where Are We Now?

Many concepts used by the Japanese to secure this favorable trend
have been adopted by U.S. manufacturers and others throughout the
world; however, U.S. companies and others have also developed
innovative approaches of their own. It has become a matter for debate
as to the present relation of the trend lines indicated in Figure 11.1. A
best estimate would be that the quality of some U.S. products lag,
whereas others are equal to the Japanese or, in a few cases, even better. The issue is somewhat clouded by the number of Japanese-owned
plants in the United States and by the increased number of U.S.-
owned plants worldwide. As in the past, each company must prove,
and then continue to improve, its own position in the marketplace.

Eliminating Threats to Quality

In the planning process, a purchasing organization may identify situations in which available suppliers are not able to meet projected requirements. The projected deficiencies may occur in capacity, cost, or quality. Where these threats to future requirements are identified, the firm has certain options:

1. Look for new sources
2. Provide selected suppliers with financial or technological assistance
3. Develop internal capability
4. Motivate suppliers to develop their own additional capability

During the early 1980s, progressive U.S. firms tended to implement a combination of the second and fourth options as a partnership-like strategy of working closely with certain suppliers to furnish long-term needs.

Many firms now have found ways of improving quality of supplier's products and lowering costs. The trend has been to place reliance on suppliers that historically have provided quality products rather than on sampling techniques designed to determine quality for acceptance or rejection of individual deliveries. One way of accomplishing this has been to change the strategy of dealing with suppliers from one of hostility to one of working together more closely. This has resulted in supplier strategies that do the following:

1. Involve suppliers early in the development of new products
2. Give suppliers improved forecasts of both short-term and long-term needs
3. Decrease the number of suppliers for each part or material to a few sources that consistently have shown the ability to furnish quality

4. Decrease the number of suppliers further by procuring several items from one source (The total reduction in number of suppliers from strategies 3 and 4 combined may be as high as a factor of ten to one.)
5. Work more closely with each supplier to achieve certification and ensure the ability to furnish quality products consistently
6. Reduce inventories of purchased goods
7. Eliminate or reduce the necessity for inspection of goods upon receipt
8. Enter into long-term contracts (three to five years or more)
9. Help suppliers implement statistical and/or computerized process controls
10. Develop a part-evaluation team that uses preproduction assessments at various points in the process to identify problems.

Benefits Achieved

By reducing the number of suppliers and giving those retained a long-term commitment, buyers permit suppliers to install more efficient manufacturing and inspection equipment and to invest in skilled personnel. Both these factors result in long-term cost reductions and quality improvements, to the benefit of both the selling and buying organization.

These strategies have resulted in cost savings in the following ways:

1. Fewer lots are rejected and returned to the supplier.
2. Inspection upon receipt at buyer's facility can be reduced or eliminated.
3. Rework or repair related to use of defectives in assembly can be reduced.

4. Inventory costs are reduced, as lots are delivered as needed for manufacturing.
5. Paperwork formerly needed in handling rejected material is reduced.
6. Warranty costs and other service costs incurred after products are delivered to the final user are reduced.

Results May Take Time

Companies planning to change their procurement strategy to incorporate these ideas should not expect immediate results. Japanese firms and U.S. firms that have achieved results with these strategies have spent several years accomplishing them. They will involve an investment in time and money, with returns not immediately evident. However, this must not be a reason for procrastination, and some results should become apparent quickly.

> **Case Example.** A supplier provided the plastic case for a customer's product. Deliveries were being made every other day in quantities of three thousand (one thousand of each for three part numbers). Receiving inspection was based on a sampling plan. Because of lot rejections, 100 percent inspection was initiated prior to use on the production line. Receiving inspection had rejected an average of 18 percent of the lots. In addition, 2 to 3 percent of the items were rejected from the subsequent 100 percent inspection. The supplier's initial response was to provide sorting prior to sending the material while studying the condition. The rejections by the customer and interruptions in the production line continued for several months, with occasional signs of improvement but not real improvement occurring.
>
> The quality manager at the customer's facility summarized the supplier's performance from a quality, delivery, and cost standpoint. The material was between 2 to 8 percent defective. Delivery to the floor was late 15 to 20 minutes on

three out of five days per week, and lost sales directly attributed to the parts exceeded $1000 per day (over $250,000 annually). Supplier's management was invited to review the information and as a result, the plant manager at the supplier's facility brought the entire staff together for a review. The customer was asked to allow them two weeks to evaluate the situation, at which time a meeting would be held.

The first meeting was attended by the customer's and supplier's plant managers and their entire staff. At the meeting, the supplier's quality manager summarized the rejections, identifying the highest to lowest rates of occurrences (a Pareto analysis). He then listed the likely causes in each category. In the presentation, the supplier pointed out that the majority of the problems were due to processes or equipment, and a program for correcting each of these was identified. In addition, the supplier showed that about 20 percent of the problems were due to miscommunications and differences in interpretation. The supplier made a commitment to eliminate all their defects in four months and asked the customer to commit resources to resolving the communication problems and differences in interpretation. The customer agreed, and periodic meetings were set. Primary responsibilities were assigned. The supplier provided weekly written progress reports and maintained the assigned regular meetings. The target to achieve zero defects was achieved in three months instead of four because of the combined dedication to the effort.

The Business Process

A key element in obtaining quality products from suppliers is to identify and improve upon the business process or processes for each supplier. Here it is important to differentiate between a business process and a production process. A *production process* consists of the activities related to hardware that occur prior to product completion. A *business process* consists of a group of logically related tasks that use the resources of the organization to provide defined results in support of the organization's objectives.[1] These processes would include all service and engineering processes, customer-order processing, payroll, and others that support production. The sequence of events by which suppliers are selected and purchase orders are placed could be considered a process. Under this concept, about everything done in an organization can be considered a process and thus is subject to a continuing need for improvement. In some ways, the whole supplier's organization can be considered a component of the process. Many concepts proven successful in manufacturing or production processes are now being successfully applied to business processes and to a company as a whole. Purchasing often helps bring about changes in the supplier's business processes or in changes to the supplier's product cycle.

Steps in the Product Cycle for Purchasing

Product concept: Identify the technologies important to meeting the product-design concepts. Which of these are new? Identify potential sources for the parts and new technologies. Establish basic supplier plan and logistics.

Product design: Develop a supplier process. Evaluate variability and identify weaknesses. Locate sources for raw materials.

Design evaluation: Approve supplier process and identify process inconsistencies. Verify transportation routes. Verify every step of the process.

Design reevaluation: Prove that supplier changes improve yields; set quality standards.

Pilot runs: Make small engineering and production runs to evaluate design and process concepts.

Preproduction run: Supplier participates in the preproduction run in order to identify potential improvements in customer and supplier process or product.

---

1. H. James Harrington, *Business Process Improvement* (New York: McGraw-Hill, 1991), 9.

Pilot run: Evaluate first piece samples; make measurements and record for future use.

Production run: Monitor performance and expect the supplier to correct problems immediately.

Feedback and corrective action: Provide accurate recording of the facts and in-depth analysis of deviations; make improvements where necessary.

Evaluation and customer acceptance: Measure reliability and ease of use.

Long-Term Relationships

Management consultant Peter F. Drucker has stated that we could learn only two important things from Japanese management: (1) an effective program cannot be built on adversarial relations and (2) responsible employees can be created by giving them responsibilities. These same concepts can be applied to suppliers. First, collaboration with suppliers, rather than adversity, can lead to effective programs; and second, responsible suppliers can result from delegation of more responsibility to them.

Both buyers and suppliers need the stability and security provided by establishing long-term relationships. These relationships must be built up through efforts of both purchaser and suppliers. Each must make concessions to the other to arrive at a relationship satisfactory to both. Continuing coordination and cooperation are important in retaining the relationship once it is established.

Why have firms—which for so long strongly emphasized price competition—changed direction to place greater emphasis on the long-term relationship?

1. They have found that this results in fewer quality problems and fewer missed delivery dates.
2. When there is a supply/shortage problem, the firms with the long-term relationship suffer less than the opportunistic buyers.
3. Product quality is better when the supplier senses the potential loss of a relationship developed over time.

4. Frequent changes in suppliers require renewed periods of learning to work together.
5. Product innovations result in design changes. Implementation of changes in requirements is less costly and time-consuming when a long-term relationship has been developed.
6. If either party runs into a financial crisis, concessions are more likely if a long-term relationship exists.
7. Cooperation helps minimize inventory carrying costs.
8. Last, but not least, the firm and its suppliers can work together to solve technical problems to achieve quality improvement in the products.

However, precautions must be taken to avoid a drift into a complacent atmosphere. A buyer can reinforce the positive aspects of this strategy by using certain tactics over the life of the relationship:

1. Performing supplier audits
2. Keeping records of supplier's quality
3. Continually checking with other potential suppliers for cost quotations
4. Changing suppliers or going to second sources when the evidence indicates the need for change

However, some U.S. companies ran into difficulties in the 1970s when collaborative relationships with suppliers were abandoned.[2]

Stronger commitments to suppliers over the long term do not diminish the importance of certain other factors. The doors should be left open for new suppliers when new technologies are applicable to company products. Suppliers in turn are expected to contribute cost-cutting ideas and they are expected to understand the goals, products, and needs of the company.

2. *Business Week*, 16 February 1981, 53.

Just-in-Time

Many companies are merging the just-in-time concept with the long-term relationship in formulating procurement strategy. To review, this concept achieves the objectives of low (or no) inventory along with few (or no) defects in supplied goods. Under the just-in-time concept as used widely in Japan, goods in relatively small quantities (such as a week's supply) are sent directly to the production line with little or no incoming inspection. A prerequisite is the certified supplier—usually under a long-term working agreement—who can be depended upon to control quality and furnish defect-free goods.

Several other considerations, however, are important in the implementation of this dual strategy of just-in-time and long-term certified suppliers, as follows:

1. *Geographic proximity.* It is much easier to control transit times if the supplier's plants are close to the using facility. This is common in Japan, where Toyota, for example, has most of its suppliers within sixty miles of the assembly plant.
2. *Reliable transportation.* This may involve the provision of some purchaser-owned vehicles in case of labor stoppages.
3. *Efficient logistics.* The supplier's ability to deliver goods to the point of usage efficiently and without damage is essential.
4. *Reduced number of suppliers.* Because of the investment needed in time and dollars, a reduction in the total number of suppliers becomes a necessity.
5. *Broader knowledge by purchasing personnel.* This is especially true in the area of quality control.
6. *Centralization of purchasing.* In some cases, multidivision firms have assigned to a single plant the overall responsibility for purchase of particular parts used throughout the corporation. This responsibility could include requirements definition, procurement, and quality assurance.

Certification of Suppliers

Many firms have integrated a *supplier product certification program* into their strategy. This program consists of the following:

1. A thorough review of suppliers' quality control capabilities
2. Evaluating suppliers' capability based on projected order sizes
3. Working with suppliers to help them develop capabilities
4. Communicating the importance of quality goals
5. Obtaining acceptance of quality requirements through participation by the suppliers in establishing the requirements
6. Identifying critical components of supplied products
7. Performing an analysis of what might go wrong with products and what the effect would be
8. Assuring feedback of quality information to supplier from buyer

Those suppliers who meet exacting standards are certified to supply specific parts. This program is then a prerequisite to just-in-time supply programs.

Automation

Computer-based measuring devices have been developed in recent years. Their use permits (1) measurement of parts rapidly and with a high degree of accuracy, (2) integration of the measurement into the manufacturing process, and (3) charting the measurements to determine process patterns. This allows the manufacturer to move in the direction of totally eliminating production of defective items.

Motivating Suppliers

The benefits of improved quality would seem sufficient to cause a supplier to adopt the measures necessary to achieve the improved quality. Some, apparently, think that their companies are different and don't need such measures. In cases where additional motivation is needed, then, it can be achieved through both active and reactive means. The active motivation includes monetary recognition through exclusive contract awards, premium payments for product quality, or special payments for the supplier to carry an inventory. Nonmonetary recognition includes supplier awards or letters to management. Reactive means that may be classified as monetary include product returns, cancellation of contracts, collection of rework and scrap charges, or legal action. Nonmonetary reactive means include letters to management, on-site reviews, discrediting of quality image through press releases, and *alerts*, or disapproved product lists.

Exclusive Contract Award

Releasing exclusive contract awards to vendors who meet specific quality and delivery objectives is one method of rewarding a supplier. It represents an important motivator. For the purchaser, it reflects confidence and trust in the ability and capability of a supplier to furnish consistently high-quality products on schedule. For the supplier, besides the assurance of continuing business associated with good performance, it provides prestige and leads to additional business. The exclusive award can provide incentive payments for both quality and delivery performance. It also provides the purchaser opportunities to make a long-term contract and potentially preclude impacts of inflation by making advance purchases of material. If the supplier continues to demonstrate delivery and quality performance, the buyer's problems are reduced.

Premium Payments

Another incentive is a monetary recognition for performance. The reward should be commensurate with the effort required to meet preestablished goals. If the goals are either too easily obtained or impossible to achieve, program effectiveness is undermined. Both the buyer and supplier must agree to the criteria for determining premium payment. The expectations, both in delivery and quality performance, must be measurable and preestablished. Then they must be measured on a timely basis and reported so each side can understand the progress.

Premium payments could include payment for overtime, the cost of special equipment, prepayment for long lead material, bonuses based on delivery and quality performance, and preplanned purchase of overages. If it is successful, both the buyer and seller have much to gain from this type of program. There are dangers, however, in this approach. Why pay extra to a supplier for providing just what the contract requires anyway? A company using a premium payment plan will need to consider complacent attitudes that may develop if the plan is used.

Supplier Awards

Supplier awards, though not monetary, are important to both supplier and user. They are a demonstration to other suppliers, and also a reflection of the buyer's and seller's quality. For both buyer and supplier, the awards provide a level of prestige and community recognition and an intangible measure of performance. When presented, the award should involve ceremony consistent with the award's significance. If it is a major national award, a press release should appear in an appropriate national newspaper. Releases in local newspapers are also important recognition of the performance. The ceremony should include top-level management from both the buyer's and supplier's facilities and, most importantly, participation by members of the work force.

Letters to Management

Although not as prestigious as supplier awards, letters to management play important roles in granting recognition for individuals or organizations that achieve goals or put forth special effort. Those receiving the letters of recognition should be deserving, and all individuals involved should be identified.

Return of Goods

Unless a buyer returns defective material to the supplier, the buyer may be establishing a level of acceptable quality. In other words, if a user continually accepts lots of materials that have defects or that include defective items, the supplier has little initiative to correct a problem. In fact, the supplier is led to believe that the quality provided is totally acceptable for use. If the supplier receives no communication from the user about defects, there is an implied revision to the specification concerning the quality as well as the design requirements for the product.

Product returns have several effects on the supplier. First, they result in a debit of sales to be issued to the supplier and become noticeable as extra expense due to the shipping costs incurred. In some cases, shipping and handling costs are more expensive than the material returned. Product returns provide the supplier with firsthand evidence of the quality required by the user as well as firsthand evidence of the defective material. Product returns also result in lost productivity due to the fact that they require rework in the factory and additional handling and cost. Returning products may also ensure management's attention at the user's facility, since the return could result in low levels of productivity. Here, the user must audit product-return and product-acceptance practices to ensure that implied specification revisions are not occurring through continued use of defective material through material review board actions.

Contract Cancellation

Cancellation of a contract due to poor quality or performance is a reaction to continuing problems with a supplier and a perception that the supplier is unable to correct the problem. Cancellation of the contract, if based on poor quality performance, may have a heavy monetary impact on the supplier, since material may have been purchased for use in fulfilling the contract, and work may be in process. These parts may not be usable for any other contract the supplier has. In addition, the cancellation creates a problem of work force instability for the supplier, especially if the contract represented a sizable portion of the business.

This action usually reflects a user's assessment that the supplier is unable to correct serious quality deficiencies that exist in the processing of products at the supplier's facility. Generally, the user doesn't desire the cancellation any more than the supplier, since the user is then faced with developing an alternate method of obtaining the material or process. It may mean program delays or line shut-downs at the user's facility. However, obtaining an alternative supplier may be the user's only method of achieving acceptable product performance.

Charging the Supplier

An incentive that users often do not use is the charging of rework and scrap to the supplier, either by direct invoicing or reduction of pay-ments on incoming invoices. The rework and scrap charges involved at the user's facilities may be a substantial portion of the original invoice amount. The fact that a charge is being made to the supplier for rework or scrap incurred by the user generally involves the buyer to the extent that the charge must be negotiated with the supplier. In addition, it brings the defect to the attention of both the buyer and supplier and emphasizes the impact of the defect on the user's sys-tem. It represents another communication method that could poten-tially result in corrective action efforts at the supplier's facility to ensure that additional charges will not be incurred for future defective material. The supplier may choose to perform the rework to minimize the charge involved. However, due to production constraints, the user may insist that rework be accomplished at the user's facility by first sorting the material and then repairing the defective material at the supplier's facility. If sorting is accomplished by the supplier at the user's facility, significant travel costs may be involved, which will affect the overall profits of the supplier. Going still further, where the nonconforming supplier part is the cause of a problem, the supplier can be billed for the costs related to shutdown production lines, sort-ing the good items from rejected lots, and removal of defective parts from assemblies.

Even if an acceptable rework or scrap charge to the supplier can-not be negotiated by the buyer, information concerning the levels of rework and scrap resulting from a defective product allows for nego-tiation of reduced cost on a new product or a product yet to be shipped. The amount and number of charges made for poor quality performance resulting in rework or sorting at the user's facility become a measure for the buyer in determining whether future contracts might better be awarded to a higher-cost bidder. In this case, a lack of responsiveness by the supplier could result in loss of contracts for new business.

Threat of Litigation

Legal action may be the most undesirable way of achieving resolution of a supplier-user problem, since it is time-consuming, costly, and unpredictable. Neither the supplier nor the user can be assured of the judgment that will be made in court. Quite often, there are documentation conflicts in contracts and contract clauses resulting in legal decisions not satisfactory to either side. Although they are a burden to both the user and supplier, legal actions should be used if the situation calls for such action. Essentially, the contemplation of legal action is an incentive to try to resolve the problem by other means.

On-Site Representative at Supplier's Facility

Stationing a user's representative at the supplier's facility could result in some loss of manufacturing control by the supplier. The supplier's flexibility in production as well as personnel usage become constrained by the presence of an on-site representative. Moreover, on-site representatives generally require additional technical support not planned for by the supplier. Their presence can be positive, however, if the representatives work to establish better communication channels between the supplier and the user and to reduce difficulties as they arise. The on-site individual can be used to interpret specifications as well as to expedite interpretations of contract requirements by contacting user's employees not generally available to the supplier.

Other types of on-site reviews could involve a visit by several user's representatives—including purchasing, quality control, manufacturing, or other technical representatives. This review team could become the impetus for a stringent audit of supplier's facilities and processes to determine quality approach as well as conformance to requirements. However, an interruption of the daily flow of products, as well as of production, could result—especially if supplier-user communications are strained. In the right atmosphere, though, visits can be positive. User's problems and lack of correlation of techniques could be uncovered and resolved during the visit, and supplier's systems proven to be acceptable from a product and quality standpoint could be discovered. In general, however, the underlying threat of on-site visits is a motivation to the supplier to seek solutions to problems beforehand.

Motivation and Long-Term Relationships

In the relationship between a firm and its suppliers, there are two ways in which motivation for quality can be obtained under the teamwork concept.

1. The continuance of the long-term relationship in itself furnishes a motivation for the supplier to provide quality in the products or services.
2. The experienced firm can assist the supplier in the implementation of concepts that have proved successful in improving quality and productivity. The firm can supply film presentations to the supplier, which can be shown to personnel at all working levels. These presentations would show how the products are used and the importance of furnishing products without defects, which will perform properly when placed in use.

The theory Z concept of management also fits well with the motivation for quality and the strategy for long-term relationships with suppliers. Dr. William G. Ouchi defines a way of managing people that focuses on a strong company commitment, a policy of retaining long-term employees, very careful evaluation of employees prior to promotion, development of managers to operate in several functional areas, consensus decision making, and close communications.[3]

Quality problems often result from the inability of someone at the supplier's facility to obtain an answer to a question, such as a question about interpretation of a requirement. Some firms have hot lines through which anyone at the supplier facility can call and ask a question. The inability to obtain an answer to a question greatly undermines motivation. Also, a response to a question often results in clarification or even a requirement change.

The objective of a motivation program is to arrive at a position where supplier's personnel accept responsibility for quality. This depends on letting the supplier have some latitude in deicing how requirements are to be achieved. The primary motivation to the supplier is the expectation of continuing business over an extended period of time as long as quality products are supplied, on schedule, and at a competitive price.

In any quality plan, we come back to the fact that the responsibility for quality rests with the purchasing organization. Other parts of the organization have a part to play, but purchasing must take over and administer the strategy to achieve quality from suppliers.

3. William G. Ouchi, *Theory Z: How American Business Can Meet the Japanese Challenge* (Reading, PA: Addison-Wesley, 1981).

Index